TWAYNE'S WORLD AUTHORS SERIES

A Survey of the World's Literature

Sylvia E. Bowman, Indiana University

GENERAL EDITOR

GERMANY

Ulrich Weisstein, Indiana University

EDITOR

Ernst Barlach

(*TWAS 26*)

TWAYNE'S WORLD AUTHORS SERIES (TWAS)

The purpose of TWAS is to survey the major writers —novelists, dramatists, historians, poets, philosophers, and critics—of the nations of the world. Among the national literatures covered are those of Australia, Canada, China, Eastern Europe, France, Germany, Greece, India, Italy, Japan, Latin America, New Zealand, Poland, Russia, Scandinavia, Spain, and the African nations, as well as Hebrew, Yiddish, and Latin Classical literatures. This survey is complemented by Twayne's United States Authors Series and English Authors Series

The intent of each volume in these series is to present a critical-analytical study of the works of the writer; to include biographical and historical material that may be necessary for understanding, appreciation, and critical appraisal of the writer; and to present all material in clear, concise English—but not to vitiate the scholarly content of the work by doing so.

Ernst Barlach

By EDSON M. CHICK

Twayne Publishers, Inc.   ::   New York

For Barbara, Edson, Pete, Sue, and Amy

Preface

I have tried to present a rounded, coherent picture of Ernst Barlach (1870–1938), the writer. A discussion of his sculpture and graphic work, for which he is best known in this country, would only obscure the view of his plays and novels. My aim is to win sympathetic readers for a dramatist of the first rank, whom German critics have long recognized as the equal of any writer of his time.

Barlach's diction is such that few translators have ventured to search for English equivalents. Alex Page took the risk. However, his workmanlike rather flat translations give only an inkling of the original. In striving for clarity, he tends to obscure the verbal texture, color, humor, and grotesquery.

This study seeks to emphasize these qualities. At its heart are four chapters, each of which closely interprets a single play from a different standpoint and with reference to the whole body of Barlach's work and thought. The remaining three chapters—on his life, his attitude toward the past, and the staging of his plays—serve much the same function. Chapter 1 is an intellectual biography which relates Barlach's experiences and opinions to his work. And the fate of Barlach in the theater teaches us a great deal about the peculiar qualities of his style.

The book may seem overloaded with footnotes. I have chosen this method of documentation in preference to more distracting parentheses. And I wanted to let Barlach speak for himself as much as possible. Unfortunately, he has to do so through the medium of my translations. These are the abbreviations used in the notes:

Briefe, I = *Aus seinen Briefen,* ed. Friedrich Dross. Munich, 1947.

Briefe, II = *Leben und Werk in seinen Briefen,* ed. Friedrich Dross. Munich, 1952.
Briefe, III = *Frühe und späte Briefe,* eds. Paul Schurek and Hugo Sieker. Hamburg, 1962.
Dramen   = *Das dichterische Werk, Vol. I: Die Dramen.* Munich, 1956.
Prosa, I   = *Das dichterische Werk, Vol. II: Die Prosa I.* Munich, 1958.
Prosa, II = *Das dichterische Werk, Vol. III: Die Prosa II.* Munich, 1959.
Gespräch = *Barlach im Gespräch,* aufgezeichnet von Friedrich Schult. Wiesbaden: Insel-Verlag, 1948.

Piper & Co. have generously allowed me to quote in translation from their editions of Barlach's works and letters.

I wish to thank the editors of the *Germanic Review, Modern Language Quarterly, Modern Language Review,* and *German Quarterly* for their permission to adapt articles, which first appeared in their journals, for use in this book. The footnotes give detailed documentation and acknowledgements.

My thanks also to Professors Werner Hollmann of Princeton and the late Walter Muschg of Basel for introducing me to Barlach; to the Fulbright Commission for a research year in Hamburg; to the *Barlach-Gesellschaft* and the *Theatersammlung der Freien und Hansestadt Hamburg* for permission to use their archives; to Virginia L. Close of Dartmouth's Baker Library for help in getting at sources; to Dartmouth's Committee on Research for defrayal of incidental expenses; to the Humanities Division of the University of California, Riverside, the Harpur College Humanities Conference, and the *Studenten-Verbindung Germania* for listening and responding to parts of this book; and to Ortrun Gauthier for clerical and editorial help far beyond the call of duty.

EDSON M. CHICK

Dartmouth College

Contents

Contents

Chronology

1870 Ernst Barlach born in Wedel (down the Elbe from Hamburg) on January 2.

1884 Death of his father.

1888 Studied at the Institute for Applied Art (*Gewerbeschule*), Hamburg.

1891 Studied sculpture at the Dresden Academy.

1895 In Paris at the Académie Julian.

1896 In Friedrichroda with his mother.

1897 Five months in Paris.
Worked as a sculptor in Hamburg and Altona.

1899 Sculpture and graphic work in Berlin.

1901 Lived alone in Wedel.

1904 Taught at the School for Ceramics at Höhr.

1905 Back in Berlin.

1906 Birth of his son Nicolaus. Trip to Russia.

1907 Berlin. Won lawsuit for custody of Nicolaus. Member of the Berlin Secession. Contract with Paul Cassirer.

1909 Fellowship to the Villa Romana in Florence.

1910 Took up residence in Güstrow (Mecklenburg) with his mother and son.

1912 Published *Der tote Tag* (*The Dead Day*).

1915 In the German army for two and a half months.

1918 Published *Der arme Vetter* (*The Poor Relation*).

1919 Member of the Berlin Academy of Arts. Turned down two offers of professorships.

1920 Mother's suicide. Published *Die echten Sedemunds* (*The Genuine Sedemunds*).

1922 Published *Der Findling* (*The Foundling*).

1924 Published *Die Sündflut* (*The Flood*) and received the Kleist Prize for it.

1926   Published *Der blaue Boll* (*The Blue Mr. Boll*).

1928   Published *Ein selbsterzähltes Leben* (*A Self-Told Life*).

1929   Published *Die gute Zeit* (*The Good Time*).

1933   Decorated with the order Pour le mérite.

1934   The Magdeburg War Memorial removed and stored.

1936   Sculptures removed from an exhibition at the Berlin Academy of Arts. A volume of drawings confiscated by the *Gestapo*.

1937   Barlach officially labelled a "decadent" artist. Kiel memorial removed. Güstrow memorial removed and later melted down.

1938   Barlach dies at a clinic in Rostock on October 24. Buried in Ratzeburg on October 28.

CHAPTER 1

The Phases of Becoming

IN writing a sketch of Ernst Barlach's life, the first obstacle one meets is the artist's reticence about personal matters. To be sure, he composed conscientious thoughtful letters to friends and strangers. He seems to have used his correspondence as others might an intellectual discussion, to work out his views on world affairs, art, and the human condition. Perhaps more biographical information will come to light when a complete edition of his letters appears. The three volumes now in print are incomplete. Also, the Barlach archives hold other material, such as prose sketches and fragments of plays, to fill more volumes. Barlach kept a diary during World War I, but this too is of little help; for, as always, he merely alludes to important events in his life and then generalizes from them. Anyone relying on published material, then, can only give the barest hints about his complicated relationships to his illegitimate son, the latter's mother, Barlach's own mother, his publisher Paul Cassirer, his business manager Böhmer, Mrs. Böhmer, Theodor Däubler, Albert Kollmann, and many others of whom he writes and whom he knew well.

The situation is doubly aggravating because these relationships, more than anything else, form the experiential substance Barlach exploited for his plays and novels. He was not a bookish man. Very little of his writing or sculpture is derivative. His sources were personal experience and observation—in Russia, on the streets of Hamburg, Wedel, Berlin, and Güstrow, in his home, and in intellectual intercourse with his contemporaries. "I have taken all my stuff from the street, not out of museums or from the Academy," he said in his last years.[1]

Even his *Ein selbsterzähltes Leben* (*Self-Told Life*, 1928) frustrates the biographer, firstly, because it describes only selected events in an oblique and highly stylized manner and, secondly, because it covers nothing beyond 1911, when Barlach had just come into his own. It simply ignores the seventeen intervening years of mature creativity and recognition. Yet *Ein selbsterzähltes Leben* is invaluable, for it offers Barlach's last well-made version of the spiritual autobiography, fragments of which form the basis of his other writings. It does not take the form of a continuous narrative but rather moves abruptly from station to station on the tortuous path leading from isolated memories of childhood to the point where the way becomes free and open. What comes after this emergence is of small interest to Barlach. It offers no challenge. As in his plays and novels, he seeks to rescue this life from the realm of immediate experience and raise it to the clearer airs of observation, to transform his life into something distinctly visible and place it in proper perspective.

This is the aim of *Ein selbsterzähltes Leben,* and it is also its dominant theme. Barlach tells us how he learned to see and how he acquired his creative vision. One could say that the plays, and perhaps the sculpture too, are likewise open-ended. They point to something beyond themselves.

For still another reason the story ends where Barlach's career begins. He is constantly concerned with growth and becoming. In his significant writing, he shows how the seeds germinate, not how the flower blossoms. The end, for Barlach, always marks a fresh beginning. In 1932, looking back over his life, he writes in a letter, "I have now very nicely got past my sixtieth year and conceive of life more than ever as an incessant process whose impetus has scarcely slackened and is my secret and greatest joy. Through this process all my earlier struggles turn into phases, each one of which I passed through with absolute conviction, but none of which I can view as my last and utmost. . . . To stand fast in stable possession would seem deplorable to me. The risk of ruthlessness must be taken." [2] Another passage from the same letter underscores the Faustian quality of this life view: "One day the hour will strike when the point of no progress is reached. I don't wish to have to hear it."

In letters written in 1925, Barlach expresses his whole world view through the word "phase." ". . . but the whole setup [this world] seems to me meaningful and practical only when viewed as a stage, as a phase, as a poorly ventilated, narrow pass where

everything is poorly organized." And later: "In the end, the concept of time becomes problematic and one sees in life only the
break-through phase into the next condition. In this perspective,
all disharmonies dissolve and become necessary elements of the
single great harmony of existence." [3]

Thus Barlach links—here discursively, elsewhere poetically—
his ideas of perspective and becoming. His dramas, novels, and
prose sketches seek to crystallize timeless, nearly ineffable transi-
tions, be they in the maturing of an artist or of a more general
spiritual nature.

I *Boyhood and Early Trials*

Ernst Barlach was born on January 2, 1870, in Wedel near
Hamburg. His father, Dr. Georg Barlach, was a general practi-
tioner in Wedel and subsequently in Schönberg and Ratzeburg,
towns in Holstein. In his autobiography, Barlach recalls a series of
episodes from his early and happy years. His father, for instance,
allowed his sons—Ernst had twin brothers younger than himself
—"to participate in his practice, which was carried on by horse
and buggy—and once I really came to the end of the world. I
knew for sure that this roaming through spaceless darkness took
place at the edge of reality, and I had plenty of time to ponder
without distraction the obviousness of the improbable, for there
was never any talking on these trips into the countryside." [4]

Young Ernst absorbed a lot from his father; for, he writes, "I
think the best education lies in the example of worthwhile activ-
ity, and children have, aside from eyes and ears, many other receptive organs." [5]

Family life was disrupted in these years when his mother
suffered a nervous breakdown, not her last, and had to leave home
temporarily. Then his father died in 1884. The cryptic, taciturn,
almost bitter description of this event furnishes only a hint of
what it meant to Ernst then and later.

Dr. Barlach died of pneumonia contracted on one of those calls
to the country. Barlach writes of his father's last days:

His colleagues saw in the whole affair an occasion for a whimsical
council by the sickbed, came and went, consulted a bit, and laughed
aloud at this pneumonia business, puffed the room full of smoke, and

then stayed away to a man when the illness failed to respond to this kind of treatment. My mother was called. Uncle Karl, a doctor in Neumünster, hastened to us and said to me one morning, while brushing his teeth with vehemence, "Ernst, things look bad for your father," —and drove off because he had serious cases to tend to in his own practice.

The doctor had no doctor.

On the Thursday after Pentecost I was called and had to watch as a debt was called in too soon, a debt which a man did not recognize and which was cruelly collected.[6]

At age eighteen, after some hesitation, Ernst left school—in effect a decision against an academic or professional career—and enrolled in a school of applied art in Hamburg. There followed almost eighteen years of seemingly aimless wandering from place to place and school to school. He taught and studied sculpture, ceramics, and drawing in Dresden, Paris, Friedrichroda (Thuringia), Wedel, and Berlin. In these rootless journeyman years he produced nothing of consequence. Referring to the drawings of this time, he writes in 1924, "I can view almost all of them, in fact everything completed before 1906, only with the admission that my case was hopeless. They show nothing but immeasurably good intentions, totally adolescent enthusiasm, romanticism, lack of direction, and the meagerest sense for calm and simplicity."[7] Through hard work, however, he did acquire a remarkable manual skill, and his specialty was the forming of details such as elaborate folds in large sculptures, one of which, a giant Neptune, went to adorn the Hamburg-America Line building in Hamburg.

Barlach's remarks about his sculpture and drawings apply equally well to the writings from these years. Some prose sketches, poems, and the fragment of a novel have been published posthumously in *Prosa I,* but their value is largely documentary. They are characterized by painfully forced whimsy, overladen allegory, and simplistic personification. The novel fragment bears the title "Humor and the Spirit of Observation Take a Trip."

Throughout his life, Barlach cultivated his threefold talent for sculpture, drawing, and writing. He wrote to his friend Düsel in 1889, "Now sculpture can't satisfy me altogether; therefore I draw, and because that doesn't satisfy me, I write. I have felt this urge since I was a boy; I had been happy learning to read and write, read on and on, and then wrote variations on what I had read in the form of plays and stories." [8] His head was always full of plots and scenes, and he succumbed often to the temptation of writing. Sculpture earned him a living but his first love was the drama. For instance, he writes of work on the play entitled *Der arme Vetter* (*The Poor Relation*): "I have again taken up work on a drama . . . that is, in the end, instinctively my surest talent." [9]

From his earliest Cooperesque Indian stories to his last absurd anti-novel, *Der gestohlene Mond* (*The Stolen Moon*), Barlach was obsessed with the power and impotence of words. "Words," he writes in 1932, "are useless, at best a crutch for those who are content to hobble. And yet there is something in words that penetrates to the inmost essence, when they come from purity and absolute truth. . . . I have long since tired of words, but they keep coming back to my lips." [10] Words are mysterious, ambiguous, protean things, but for this very reason they "may reach to the limits of the absolute." Drama and narrative can say things which a piece of sculpture will not express.

In his *Ein selbsterzähltes Leben*, Barlach brings the resources of language to bear on the phases of his own life and on the major changes in his creative style. In the years before 1906 he did develop, even though the products may have seemed hopeless. The following passage describes what an art historian might call the transition from Naturalism to *Jugendstil* (the German term for art nouveau). For Barlach it is a distinctly human process, a change in attitude toward reality, a radical change in his mode of vision, gradual and hard to articulate.

There occurred, at some time or other during this unsuspecting wandering about, a renunciation of the uncritical acceptance of every chance form. I began . . . to be eclectic. Hesitantly enough, I began to leave things out, . . . was no longer simply tolerant and subservient to visible being. I was impudent enough to organize it, whereby my progress faltered often enough and I could do nothing but fall from the intended organization into an ornamental swing and swell. [11]

This "some time or other" might be located in the later 1890's. It precedes what Barlach calls his Wedel years, 1901–1904, which he spent living in seclusion in his native town. This is a period of crisis and despair, the darkness before the dawn and great awakening of 1906. Barlach characterizes it with words like weakness, extravagance, self-deception, and immaturity.[12]

The novel *Seespeck* treats this time in detail, and as in the case of *Ein selbsterzähltes Leben*, it is hard to separate fact from fiction. Read as a spiritual autobiography, it tells how Barlach found his true way and gave substance to his life. To summarize and anticipate a more detailed consideration in Chapter 5, the Wedel years were an end and a beginning. Seespeck—obviously an autobiographical figure—enters the period quite unsure of his identity. He is still enslaved by his eyes and their tolerant uncritical acceptance of visible being. His hunger for "eye-experiences" has transformed him into a faceless outsider, and he has become more a shadow than an individual.

In a series of basically similar episodes we see Seespeck's growing feeling of alienation from society and self. He has purposely chosen this existence but gradually becomes aware that he has turned into a shadowy spectator on the edge of life. The fictional account of his emergence from this abysmal state concentrates the long laborious transformation in a single moment. Seespeck's inner awakening is provoked by a slight change in the way the sun throws its light on a particular afternoon. The subtle optical effect changes his whole point of view.

II 1906, The Great Transformation

The novel's conclusion, a grotesquely comic episode evolving from a practical joke, does not satisfy the reader; nor did Barlach consider the work finished. In fact, he never released it for publication. Strangely, the events in his life surrounding the great breakthrough of 1906 are far more dramatic. Two things happened in this year to pull him out of the Seespeckian doldrums. First, the birth of his son gave substance to his shadow existence. Second, his trip to Russia suggested a new way of looking at man and reality.

Another quote from *Ein selbsterzähltes Leben* describes his mood during the months spent in Berlin before the turning point.

I knew I was sitting in a hell and sat there struggling every day to overcome the consciousness of my total superfluousness. . . . I scarcely had the courage to get up and would have fled back to bed at ten in the morning. I was going to ruin, and my life was ebbing as if it were being emptied like the Elbe in an easterly gale. And yet in these darkest times a young life had started on its way, as if to take my hand and lead me back into a rising existence.

It was thus no great trick to talk me into the trip to Russia . . .[13]

The life that had started on its way was Nicolaus, his only off-spring and the most important person in his life. Superficially it was for his sake that Barlach left Berlin in 1910 to settle in the small Mecklenburg city of Güstrow. But for Nicolaus, Barlach might never have settled down at all. And one can say that the boy saved him from self-destruction.

Klaus was born in 1906, and in the ensuing months Barlach was worried about the boy's welfare. His mother, he thought, was not fit to raise him. "I have decided to risk everything for his custody," he writes in 1907, "because I am convinced that his mother should not have him." [14] And so Barlach brought suit to gain custody of his illegitimate son. He won the suit late in the year 1908.

How much Barlach needed the boy we can see from general remarks in his correspondence. "The lad, together with the law-suits, has consumed everything, but I am not angry—I have no regrets—a man without children has only a fragmentary feeling for humanity and his position in the world. The resultant expansion of my whole ego through the experience of these past years is cheap at the price." And later, "I—to allude to egoistic matters—I need the boy, frankly, for my own education, as a daily warning not to let myself go in a formless, limitless life." [15]

In Barlach's case, one can speak with justification of a father-son mystique. We have already seen the beginnings of it in the account of his father's death. The plays, particularly *Der tote Tag* (*The Dead Day*), *Die echten Sedemunds* (*The Genuine Sede-munds*), and *Die Sündflut* (*The Flood*) testify more eloquently to this than does the following passage from a letter of condolence which Barlach wrote to his uncle:

I am not vain enough to believe I could say anything of value to you on the occasion of your father's death. Actually I could say so much that no letter could contain it, for the concepts father and son have for me a vast significance. . . . It may be that my experiences have infused my father concept with so much mysticism that these things are different in your eyes.[16]

Barlach lived and worked for his son Klaus with great intensity in order to compensate for having deprived the boy of his mother. Barlach's own mother was no substitute for the real thing. For nine years, the trio lived together in a state of nervous tension. In 1920 Luise Barlach drowned herself while a patient at a sanitarium.

Barlach was not always so unambiguously enthusiastic about his Russian experience as he was in 1906 on his return from a tour through Kiev, Kharkov, and other towns in the Ukraine. By 1928, when he published his *Ein selbsterzähltes Leben,* he may have sensed that his earlier remarks, which appeared in a periodical in 1912 under the title "A Trip to the Steppes," would make good source material for rightist propagandists trying to discredit him as un-German and a Bolshevik Jew.

The following comments of 1928 should be read in this light:

I find it superfluous to counter the legend that only thanks to Russia did I achieve my plastic expressiveness. . . . The fact is that reality has always been plastic reality for my eye and that I brought to Russia an unsatisfied need with me, a readiness and capacity to see—not the others—but the plastic values. Russia gave me its forms, but I suspect that I had a share in the eventual result, for when I returned and began the first two beggars—those beggars who are for me symbols for the human situation in its nakedness between heaven and earth—when I began them . . ., the old doubt cropped up: Will this finally be real sculpture or just modelling.[17]

Yet in the next paragraph he nearly contradicts himself and says that Russia gave him more than form.

. . . The following perception dawned on me: You can without hesitation risk everything you possess, the uttermost, the innermost, gestures of piety and rage; for everything, be it hellish paradise or paradisal hell, there is an expression, as in Russia one or both are realized.

When I returned home, I could see my son, and while I worked on my first clay figure, I set about working on the drama *Der tote Tag.*[18]

Der tote Tag was Barlach's first published play and, for all its weaknesses, the first step on the way to the masterpieces of the 1920's.

Barlach found in Russia the raw material congenial to his ideas on artistic expression. He speaks of revelations of the stunning unity of outer and inner reality, the symbolic essence, and expresses the conviction: "We humans are thus, at bottom, all beggers and problematic existences." [10] The Slavs allegedly reveal this where others conceal it. Thus it was clearly not Slavic culture that overpowered him as it did other German intellectuals of the time. Rilke, for instance, had traveled to Russia a few years earlier and gave expression to his enthusiasm for the Russian soul in the sentimental pseudo-mystical outpourings of his *Book of Hours* (1899–1903). Later, Hermann Hesse, too, was captivated by Russia as a cultural force. In "The Waste Land," T. S. Eliot has immortalized Hesse's vision of the barbaric invasion from the East, an apocalyptic spectacle half Spengler, half Dostoyevsky. And Thomas Mann made good use of the mysterious East cliché in *The Magic Mountain.*

For Barlach, on the other hand, the trip to Russia resulted in a creative metamorphosis. To be sure, it gave him new ideas and subjects, but the real gain was a new mode of vision. This experience, learning to see, underlies the action of his best plays; and this is what he writes of in his "Russian Journal" (1906–1907) and "A Trip to the Steppes." It is clear from these trustworthy accounts that the beggar figures he refers to are but a small part of the whole experience. For Barlach saw them—he makes this point repeatedly—against a limitless background of plain or steppe. The beggars actually form part of the infinite grotesque detail in the foreground that his hungry eyes had always devoured. "Distance," writes Barlach in the "Russian Journal," "as the distinct idea of neverendingness [Nie-Endlichkeit] was for me the essence of my experience." [20]

The two infinities—those of distance and foreground—meet at the horizon; and the horizon becomes Barlach's focal point, the locus of the human situation between heaven and earth. The earthy yet ethereal nature of the sculptures, just like the grotesquely sensual yet highly spiritual content of the dramas—and the essential unity of each—are all variations on the new "horizontal" vision. In the discussion of the plays and *Seespeck* we shall see the creative importance of this part of the Russian experience.

"A Trip to the Steppes" describes in visual terms the establishment of a dynamic inner balance and harmony between two innate tendencies Barlach observed in himself and others, not unlike the two souls which Goethe's Faust harbors in his breast. The first is the tendency to focus on the grotesqueries of the foreground, a naturalistic preoccupation with material, flesh, and appetite. The second is the tendency to abstract, to deny this world, to speculate, and to indulge his delight in the swing and swell of *Jugendstil*. His best plays—*Der arme Vetter, Die echten Sedemunds, Die Sündflut,* and *Der blaue Boll* (*The Blue Mr. Boll*)—tell of the achievement of this balance. Barlach's first play, *Der tote Tag,* and his last, *Der Graf von Ratzeburg* (*The Count of Ratzeburg*), both betray an imbalance toward abstraction and allegory.

III *Däubler and Abstract Art*

The Russian experience opened Barlach's eyes to new visual values in landscapes and in the human form. This may explain his provincial, and very un-German, remarks on how uncongenial he finds Italian scenery. In 1909 he received a grant to support him for a year at the Villa Romana in Florence. He seems to have suffered from homesickness and wrote to his friend Reinhard Piper,

If I only had that walk across the fields I used to take and could take every day in Berlin, I would feel much better—the few lines and planes and over them the colossal sky . . . are more essential and eloquent for me than this Florence down here. . . . One almost never gets out into the open, everywhere walls, cultures, always houses and culture.[21]

He is suspicious of the Germans' traditional enthusiasm for Italy. "Güstrow can well compete with a Tuscan city; its cathedral and parish church correspond more to my innate sensibilities than do marble cathedrals. And Gothic wood figures are simply revelations for me. Yes, it's a bad sign for our culture that everyone and his brother gads about Italy," writes Barlach in 1909, giving good esthetic reason why, in the next year, he settled for good in the town of Güstrow.[22]

The year in Italy was not a total loss, however, for it was there that Barlach formed his lifelong friendship with Theodor Däubler (1876–1934), the author of the three-volume epic *Das Nordlicht* (1910). While in Italy, Barlach assisted at the delivery of this monstrosity, read proof, and tried to restrain Däubler from adding to its 30,000 lines.

Neither this work nor any of Däubler's writings had the slightest influence on Barlach's work. But Däubler the man, the walking contradiction—the mountainously obese, gluttonous prophet of otherworldliness—provided a model for sculptures and drawings and became a kind of Mephistophelean alter ego. Barlach's hate-love for Däubler and what he stood for lies hidden beneath the basic conflicts of all his works. He called chapters 5 and 6 of the novel *Seespeck* Däubler chapters. Däubler appears undisguised under his own name, and Seespeck (*i.e.*, Barlach) struggles, like Jacob with the angel, with this apparition, which he recognizes as part of himself.

In a letter to a correspondent identified only as Fräulein N. N., Barlach writes: "Somewhere in me there is a rage against Däubler; I see a fraud with spirit and meaningfulness, a display of supposed depth, which horrifies and shocks me at times." And in an earlier letter to the same addressee he states: "As long as I have eyes to see with, I will have an anchor to tie me to the earth. With Däubler, one has to soar up to the beyond. And he doesn't see with his eyes. Rather, he has organs that may grasp colors and forms, but no eyes, not my kind anyway." [23]

Däubler, then, serves as the whipping boy for Barlach's own tendency to move into otherworldly realms of abstraction. In his critical essays on modern art, Däubler supported the new nonobjective styles of Picasso and Kandinsky. In a sketch entitled "Diario Däubler" (1912–14), Barlach remarks on the similarity between his friend and Picasso. It is quoted here at length because it is one of Barlach's most eloquent statements on art and literature.

He sees in Däubler an intellectual adventurer, a charlatan, giving the most mundane things a specious import and playing with reality to no particular end. The sketch ends like the echo of an argument:

Like Picasso! That is psychic geometry, theology and architectural mechanics, spiritual angles and a construction of intellectually tangled lines. But I say good night to that; the organic in nature is for me precisely the expression of inwardness; the human form is the expression of God, insofar as He broods, hides, burrows in man and behind people. Can inwardness be expressed by lines? By anything but externals? Can we, when we want to express something, give anything but expression? Can one paint inner being, can one indicate, 'That's the way it works,' and place himself mentally in the innards of inwardness . . .? Can one represent the mechanics of a clock and say: This is time, instead of showing the clockface and the running of the hands? To give form to psychic reality—one would have to show joy, pain, compassion, hope, despair, and how better than on the watch dial of the human countenance with the hand movements of its lines. . . . No . . . that is charlatanry, [and Picasso] an ornamental absolutist. I myself know the temptation: just to fit together lines and surfaces, but it's not the end, rather a stage, practice for the hand, to overcome the usual boredom. To fill paper and canvas in this way satisfies my needs at any rate because I want to give myself, in private, a concrete form consonant with my own being, because I want to divest myself of alien mannerisms. It is as if I were preparing a particular gesture for my appearance in public: that's how I'd like to stylize myself, take on such and such a character, but that is not the end; it is rather a support and agent for an essence that has yet to be; in the end I have to accomplish something human, and that is done not by mannerisms but by "content." Ultimately I could devise a private language: I would like to speak such sounds, roll the a's, b's, and c's, group them with such and such consonants, that's how I'd like to sound—fine, but when I appear before an audience, I must add sense and soul; then I can trim my letters and sounds to the limit of my capacity. In the end, the human eye, ear, and mind must be satisfied and stimulated; I can't form a world that doesn't exist; I have to express myself in understandable signs. Picasso speaks an Esperanto of his own invention and claims that the sound, the delivery, the gesture must produce the effect. The effect is only on the eye, esthetic. Emotion, soul are unmoved. A convention of new forms should be created which includes the content of human interests; a system of notation, a sign language should be agreed on.[24]

Equally eloquent and revealing is Barlach's reaction to Wassily Kandinsky's *Das Geistige in der Kunst* (1912), which is one of the major programmatic documents on abstract art. Barlach's friend and Kandinsky's publisher, Reinhard Piper, sent Barlach a copy late in 1911. Barlach responded as follows in a letter dated December 28, 1911:

. . . the book doesn't seem at all to be what one calls "well intentioned." Thus it is even less likely to open any doors in me; that is, I don't go along, out of instinct namely. There's a gaping chasm between us that couldn't be deeper. Recently, after several pages, I have had to retreat with the assertion that I am simply a barbarian. So, as a barbarian, I will believe this honest man when he says that he gets a deeper spiritual excitement from dots, spots, lines, and daubs à la pages 43 and 88, but no more than believe him and then—good-bye. We could talk a thousand years without agreeing. I am not, by the way, inexperienced, have myself had times when I sat and "created" lines. Those were the intervals, pauses, when brain and hand may have been willing, but everything else seemed stupefied.

. . . .

We must agree on a language in order to know anything at all: Someone could say the finest, most magnificent things in Chinese, and I wouldn't prick up my ears. If I am to empathize with a spiritual experience, then it must speak a language through which, in turn, I can experience the deepest, most hidden things. My mother-tongue is the most appropriate, and my artistic mother-tongue is, after all, the human figure or milieu, the object through which, or in which, man lives, suffers, rejoices, feels, thinks. I can't get around that. I can have nothing to do with an Esperanto art. Precisely the vulgar, the universally human, the age-old emotions of the race, those are the great, eternal ones. What man has suffered, can suffer, his greatness, his interests (including myth and dreams of the future), that's what I'm interested in, but my special little feelings or my very own special sensation are insignificant, are simply whim, when I move with them outside the circle of humanity. Man is egoistic, and his egoism—in the elevated and the low sense, as you will—must be involved, but page 88 or page 98 do not touch my egoism at all. . . . It is easy to say that blue means this and yellow that, but whether it has the divine power to be more than theory is questionable. If, however, colors and lines consist of human figures—or vice versa—then they have force, for they get it from the human soul.[25]

Considering the other side of the coin, Barlach recognized his own inclination to passive observation in his acquaintance Albert Kollmann (1837–1914), an art dealer who visited him occasionally. Kollmann, too, was a sort of alter ego and seems to have stood as model at least for some of Seespeck's traits, as well as for such figures as Hannis, the photographer in *Seespeck,* Hans Iver in *Der arme Vetter,* and Grete Grüntal in *Der blaue Boll.* Like Seespeck, he was a slave to his eyes and observed and absorbed all phenomena. He reacted with misanthropic disgust to what he saw. Of the random comments Barlach entered around 1912 in his notebook under the title "Konto Kollmann: *Der Apostel,*" we quote the following:

His leanness is not wretched, but rather superior; he is disgusted at the sight of a lot of meat.

Is his head a fox's head? At least it has that importunity, that eternal attentiveness, tension, turning, lurking, focusing of the eyes, following, combining, scorn for stupidity and crudity. He snaps at delicacies (intellectually speaking). His business is the world. Spies noiselessly.

. . . He lifts up the stone and uncovers in others disgusting underground passages and worms that shun the light.

Misanthropic disgust: once he patronized the soda water booth, and since then the man greets him so importunately that we either have to sneak past behind the booth or go around it in a wide arc across the street—simply to escape the greeting! [26]

IV *Recognition and Persecution*

Except for two weeks in the army as a forty-six-year-old winter recruit in 1916, Barlach fought the war as a civilian on the home front, caring for children in a day nursery, among other things. He shared the general euphoria of the first months of the war but was disillusioned sooner than most. Unlike other intellectuals, such as Hugo von Hofmannsthal, he saw no chance for rebirth or a new beginning after the debacle. The German people might be regenerated and find a new way of life, but only after a second ice age, he remarked in 1918.[27] The atmosphere of the 1920's only confirmed him in his pessimism: "The people have gone to the dogs and have absolutely no inkling of the only possible meaning of life; one could despair that they are even capable of looking beyond their bare, gluttonous, greedy, avaricious self-righteousness, to sense that a goal is anything more than stomach-stuffing and intestinal contentment." [28]

Two of Barlach's lesser dramas—*Der Findling* (1922) and *Die gute Zeit* (1929)—serve as vehicles for this sort of vitriolic social criticism. They are weak probably for this very reason. *Der Findling* is an obscure grotesque allegory dealing with human greed and cannibalism. *Die gute Zeit* excoriates the irresponsible hedonism of the 1920's. The pseudo-Christian endings—obvious allusions to the birth of Christ in the first and to the crucifixion in the second—seem forced and artificial.

Yet the 1920's were Barlach's good years. His best plays were published between 1918 and 1926. He was awarded the Kleist Prize for *The Flood* in 1924. He accepted this honor with mixed feelings; the judges gave it each year to encourage promising young talent, and Barlach was fifty-four years old. His plays were performed all over Germany. Generally, however, they enjoyed rather short runs. Some productions never got beyond the first night. Three or four, produced by the best companies in Hamburg and Berlin, were hits.

The pinnacle of Barlach's career coincides with the rise of Nazism in Germany. By 1929, reactionary organizations had labeled him un-German and Asiatic, largely because his war memorials in churches and public places were powerful expressions of human emotions like sorrow, pity, and religious transport. In other words, they failed to inspire military spirit. On viewing Barlach's angel in the Güstrow cathedral, one officer remarked, "How can a pastor let such a pacifist thing be put up?" Another, mistaking the nature of the memorial, said, "Have you ever seen a soldier do that?" [29] In fact, the figure, bearing the facial features of Käthe Kollwitz, hangs several feet from the floor in horizontal serenity.

The smear campaign against Barlach grew stronger, of course, after 1933. It is a familiar phenomenon to Americans who lived through the McCarthy time. The veterans' organization known as "Stahlhelm" and other self-appointed cultural police dictated standards. Barlach was a natural target, one of the first tests of their power.

Consequently, Nazi government officials needed to take little or no direct action. Barlach soon became a controversial figure. He was not officially or unequivocally ostracized, but the effect was the same, if not worse. Customers canceled commissions; theaters dared not produce his plays. No one—with the exception of Hermann F. Reemtsma (1892–1961), the cigarette magnate who kept Barlach alive in his last years and acquired a magnificent Barlach collection—would risk buying a sculpture for fear of being judged guilty by association.

The situation was the worse for being unclear. In 1933, for instance, Barlach received the order *Pour le mérite*, the highest possible distinction a German civilian can be awarded. Propaganda Minister Goebbels is said to have owned two Barlach statuettes, and the regime asked for some sculpture to decorate the Berlin Olympic Stadium in 1936. On the other hand, his work was included in an exhibition of decadent art.

In 1934 Reinhard Piper chose one hundred drawings from Barlach's portfolios with the intention of publishing them in book form with accompanying text. Piper showed the drawings to Wilhelm Pinder, then Professor of Art History at Munich. Pinder refused to write the commentary, allegedly because he did not want to be defamed. Paul Fechter then composed the text. But the book was officially condemned a few months after it appeared in 1935, and four thousand copies were confiscated.[30]

Barlach wasted the strength of his last years in a fight against an elusive, faceless, amorphous, ignorant, official-unofficial antagonist that blackened his name and literally poisoned his well water. As in the war years, he felt himself incapable of doing his best work or finishing plays already half completed. His letters of protest to government offices at all levels got no response. None was needed. The story of Barlach's last nine years reads like Kafka's *Trial*.

These frustrations, the removal of his works from museums, and the tearing down of his public monuments poisoned his existence. "Since there have been no more commissions, the swamp of useless busy-work has grown deeper," he writes in 1934.[31] At some point during this period, Frau von Nostitz, a niece of von Hindenburg, is said to have asked indirectly how she might offer Barlach some relief. He responded, "Offer relief? Let them buy my works!"[32] By the end of 1936 he had pretty well succumbed to what he calls "the irresistible force of a united mediocrity."[33] This is what ruined him and not, as most accounts state, the Nazi regime itself.

The Phases of Becoming

On October 24, 1938, he died of heart failure and pneumonia in a Rostock clinic. Four days later he was buried in Ratzeburg, the town of his boyhood. Only a small circle of friends attended the burial ceremony.

CHAPTER 2

The End Is the Beginning

D*ER arme Vetter* appeared in 1918, and like almost all of Barlach's plays, it is transitional and treats the themes of phase and change. Yet it merits special attention because it also marks a transition in Barlach's style. It signals the end of the old and the beginning of the new. Consequently it offers even more problems of interpretation than his other dramas. No single explanation can be tailored to fit the whole. We have the impression that one element discounts the next and feel the ground drop away from under our feet. There is only one certainty: metamorphosis. All three main characters are radically transformed, two because they yearn to be, and the third in spite of himself.

The pivotal position of *Der arme Vetter,* Barlach's second play, becomes clearer when we call to mind his first, *Der tote Tag* (1912). The former is a drama of success; the latter, of frustration and family failure. Mother, Son (they have no other names) and Kule, the supposed father, all fail in their duties to each other, and each fails himself at the crucial moment.

I Der tote Tag

This is literally Barlach's most obscure piece. Kule is blind, Mother prefers the dark, and once outside the house, Son cannot see for fog and because the sun does not shine. The stage directions specify gloom for two thirds of the play, namely Acts II, IV, and V.

The whole drama is based on a visual metaphor. Adolescent Son with his great but undeveloped capacity to see seeks to break away from Mother in order to create for the world a better visage ("Gesicht").[1] Blind Kule encourages him in this effort where he himself has failed. Kule's eyes were once eager and hungry too, but one day when the crowd of images and impressions became too large, they simply refused to function. He says, "You see, my eyes were two spiders, they sat in the web of their sockets and trapped the images of the world that fell in, trapped them and enjoyed their sweetness and delight. But the more images came, the greater was the number of those juicy with bitterness and larded with horror. Finally, since my eyes could no longer tolerate such bitternesses, they weaved the entrance closed, sat there inside, and preferred to starve and die." [2]

Opposed to Kule and Son's yearning to grow, see, and do stands Mother, a creature of darkness. As the play opens, she is seen emerging from the cellar into the great hall that serves as the scene for the entire action. In this allegory, Mother stands for the dark, dreams, static security, and the forces of blood and flesh.

Son struggles, in effect, to escape from the womb and enter the masculine world of light, intellect, and change. But it is a stillbirth. And the day on which he had hoped to emerge "hangs dead between heaven and earth." [3] Son is akin to the expressionist hero so common in plays of the 1910's and 1920's: The New Man. But he never becomes a man.

The audience sees nothing but an undifferentiated half-dark hall peopled with three undifferentiated human characters and three spirits, one of whom is invisible. Likewise, Son never sees anything outside the house. Nor can he even use his hands effectively.

The play ends as first Mother and then Son commit suicide. Thereupon Kule and the invisible Steißbart depart carrying with them a message for the world. Steißbart, whose name might be rendered "Rumpbeard," pronounces this message: "All men have their best blood from an invisible father . . . but it is odd that mankind will not learn that its father is God." [4] These are weighty words to come from such a source, and we may well ask if they are to be taken seriously.

II   Der arme Vetter

Barlach finished *Der arme Vetter* in 1912, the year in which *Der tote Tag* was published. He had begun work on it some time around 1909. In 1911 it bore the provisional title "The Easter People" ("Die Osterleute"), and he referred to it as a dramatic monstrosity, perhaps never to be completed.[5] He let it lie until, in

1917, his publisher and agent, Paul Cassirer, insisted on printing it. Barlach surrendered the manuscript, and the drama appeared in 1918. In the following year a new edition with lithographs by the author came out, and the Hamburg Kammerspiele gave it its premier performance on March 19, 1919.

The audience and the theater critics were excited by it though not unanimous in praise or condemnation. One critic left the theater "bored and discouraged," and another found the play "convincing and powerful." A newspaper review describes the spectators' reactions as follows: "The drama remained obscure to a great part of the audience. The angry ones giggled, grumbled, and raised a racket. But finally the good spirit of humanity prevailed." [6] In a letter to his cousin, Barlach tells of his amazement at the response: "I must say, I'm a little astonished that they don't take these events more calmly, the work seems weightier than I could have dreamt." [7]

The drama is not Barlach's best, but it is indeed heavily freighted. It merits close attention as a drama in itself and, because it comes at a crucial point in his literary career, as a document which reveals something of his development as a writer. In his sculpture, Barlach had long since moved beyond the two-dimensional, curvilinear intricacies of *Jugendstil*. Yet his only published drama was *Der tote Tag*, that ponderous bit of neo-romantic gloom, which enjoyed little success except, to Barlach's dismay, among psychoanalysts. [8]

Der arme Vetter takes place on an Easter Sunday along the upper Elbe. Of the twelve scenes, 1, 2, and 8 to 11 are set on the sandy heath near the river; the rest in one room or another of a small inn. The most striking outward distinctions from *Der tote Tag* lie in this realistic contemporary milieu and the colorful North German types such as Captain Pickenpack of the steamer "Primus" and customs guard Sieg. Barlach is striving here, he says in a letter, for the most genuine possible milieu to serve as a contrasting surface for the inner events which emerge and explode. [9] The world of this play is thus altogether different from the flat undifferentiated one of *Der tote Tag*.

III *Self-Interpretation*

According to one recent study, Barlach provided his dramas with explanatory "concluding commentaries." [10] Our discussion will, therefore, begin with a summary of the twelfth and final scene in order to see how much these commentaries explain and how they should be read. In this scene, Fräulein Isenbarn is forced to choose between allegiance to the corpse of the suicide Hans Iver and marriage to her worldly fiancé, Siebenmark. The following summary will give some inkling of the obstacles that lie in the way of easy interpretation.

In the barn of the inn at Lüttenbargen, Fräulein Isenbarn and Siebenmark stand before the body of Iver, who has finally succeeded in committing suicide. At first Fräulein Isenbarn refuses to speak. Siebenmark taunts her by hitting the corpse and telling it to rise again. He wants some light shed on the situation, for Iver has died and let his light go out at the worst time. Siebenmark executes a little dance around the body, screaming blasphemies like the following, which alludes to the Resurrection: "Tumbler doll ("Stehaufmännchen"), reconsider!" [11] The only response is from Fräulein Isenbarn who, rather than throw more light on things, speaks in paradoxes. It seems to her as if Iver had murdered Siebenmark; and as if she too had died. At this point, and without apparent motivation, she whispers to Siebenmark that she consents to sleep with him that night, and later to marry him. In the meantime, however, she insists on defining their relationship once and for all, "so to speak for eternity." [12]

Siebenmark promises to "take her at her word" with regard to the sleeping arrangements and the wedding, and she replies ambiguously, "Do it—it has nothing more to do with me." [13] The second "it" means not just that the whole matter no longer affects her but also that the *word* by which he takes her has lost its meaning. In a last vain attempt to find clarity, Siebenmark then embraces her. However, he cannot keep his tongue in check, and the word "Endlich" slips out. Thereupon Fräulein Isenbarn takes him at his word and echoes "Endlich!" Spoken by Siebenmark, the word is "finally." Spoken by Fräulein Isenbarn with scorn, it assumes a religious coloring and should be read "finite" as opposed to "infinite." The repetition leads to more vexing plays on words, to

Fräulein Isenbarn's "concluding commentary" (below), and to her expression of loyalty to the dead Iver.

Even though she has renounced language and the finite world, she tries to explain herself. With verbal reference to the foregoing, she says, "I sense a beginning, finally ("endlich") a beginning!" and in response to Siebenmark's request for clarification she delivers the following speech:

Must one descend into the grave to get away? No, there exists a mixture of beginning and end, clamped together. You can scoff at the end, you see it, and you don't like it, you have an interest in it, but the beginning, leave that alone, that is my property alone, that beginning which one experiences waking and sleeping at the same time, like a child on its first day. One can't tell right from left, but one is in the midst of things. In this new existence, one is immersed in something natural and self-evident, but now one has to learn to see, crawl, walk, and, after that, all the rest. God, what will come of all this! [14]

Siebenmark can now only try to draw her away to their room, where he thinks they can be reasonable, and where life is. She, however, scoffs at his "full, foaming life" and goes back to kiss the corpse.[15] In disgust Siebenmark decides to challenge her and insists that she choose between him and Iver. With ecstatic haste she chooses the corpse, raises the lantern to light its face, and the flame is quenched leaving the stage dark.

This is not the end, however. After a time the stage is once more illuminated by the light of day, and two secondary characters, Voβ and Engholm, enter, apparently returning from a funeral. We never learn whose funeral it is. The two men speak about the events in the play as if they were long past and hard to recall. They speculate on what has happened to Fräulein Isenbarn. All they have to go on is a cryptic note from her saying, "It's no longer me." She then contradicts herself by signing it with her full name, underneath which stands the designation "Maidservant of a great lord." [16] The two men begin a dispute over how this figure of speech should be construed and go off to debate the issue and a second one, namely whether they themselves are real or figurative ghosts, over a glass of grog.

Far from being a second, all-encompassing "concluding commentary," this little postlude has the effect of negating, or at least beclouding, what seemed a fairly reasonable resolution to a play which has no clearly visible human conflicts to be resolved. It leaves the audience somewhat in the position of Siebenmark, with his yearning to go somewhere else where one can be reasonable. In this connection, one understands the feelings of Barlach's auto-biographical character Seespeck in the novel of the same name. Warm from rowing across the river, he gazes at the winter sky and mutters, "The cold magnificence of this Orion-night clothes the mechanism of the ultraintelligible, but whoever looks and wonders, for him looking and wondering and even he himself become unintelligible.—But tonight I intend to drink grog." [17]

This is the trouble with Barlach's "concluding commentaries" or self-interpretations; under close inspection they elude one's grasp and lead to a kind of self-alienation. None of them is nearly as reliable or satisfying as a glass of grog. The end of *Der arme Vetter* is left open, and the final episode is not really a commentary but a dissolution, or questioning, of foregoing commentaries. The word "dissolution" is appropriate because authoritative-sounding statements made in the course of the drama are regularly dipped, as it were, in a caustic solution, in which they lose all substance. It is no accident that Voβ, in scene 1, pointedly describes himself as a manufacturer of caustic soda.

The postlude brings home the inadequacy of words and metaphors to describe rationally what happens within Fräulein Isenbarn or Siebenmark on this Easter Sunday. Not only is the religious issue obscured, but even the true-to-life milieu—the inn, the rough and ready north-German types—turns ghostlike. Voβ and Engholm threaten to become intangible and unintelligible to themselves. They are not quite sure how long ago it all happened; the temporal perspective is more blurred than in Fräulein Isenbarn's speech which mixes end and beginning; and one has the feeling that the funeral they come from could well have been their own.[18] The last concrete interpretation is offered by Engholm, who proposes the naïve theory that Fräulein Isenbarn has become a nun.

The sequential pattern of a serious remark from a seemingly venerable source followed by a platitudinous or downright scatological one to discount it fits many dialogues and whole scenes in *Der arme Vetter*. Attempts at illumination and clarification lead inevitably to new obscurity and riddles. For example, when Iver asks Voß, "Haben Sie etwas auf dem Gewissen?" Voß replies, "Auf wem? Der Gewisse dient mir zum Sitzen." [19] Also, Iver's imitation of Christ's passion is ridiculed so effectively in scene 6 that he is led to admit falsely that his suicide attempt was a hoax.

The greatest failing of Barlach criticism, and particulary criticism of *Der arme Vetter*, his been to neglect the ambiguities. Thus it has made the play appear to be a mystically vague, rather simple-minded piece. It pronounces Iver a martyred saint, Fräulein Isenbarn an angel, and Siebenmark a hopeless philistine. The play is not so simple. There is something of the werewolf in Iver; Fräulein Isenbarn, as the iron in her name and several allusions in the text imply, is as much Valkyrie as angel; and though not as obviously as in the case of other central figures like Calan (*Die Sündflut*) and Squire Boll, Siebenmark is the play's hero. [20]

Despite the persistent ambiguity and undercutting, *Der arme Vetter* is not a cynical or nihilistic work. The purposeful ambiguity is a device for Barlach's peculiar brand of alienation. It is not superimposed by dramaturgical technique but is rather built into the language, atmosphere, and structure. Although he may be masked as a lewd, drunken veterinarian dressed up as Frau Venus and leading the wild festivities in the bar at the inn, there is a God in Barlach's play. For all its grotesquery, the play is serious and carries a religious message, of which the grotesque is an essential ingredient.

The outer action is uncomplicated. An engaged couple, Fräulein Isenbarn and Siebenmark, make an excursion to the upper Elbe on Easter Sunday. We see them first alone on the open heath, and their conversation betrays the fact that all is not well. They are becoming estranged. Hans Iver, a very distraught young man, crosses their path briefly and then runs on. They themselves move away, and Frau Keferstein, a lascivious woman, appears, followed soon by Seaman Bolz. She welcomes his rude advances even though she has never laid eyes on him before; and they set off to find privacy in the dunes. In the course of his wanderings, Iver observes them as they lie together. At the end of scene 2, as Frau Keferstein and Bolz are taking leave of each other, they hear a gunshot. Iver has shot himself in the chest. They carry him to the inn at Lüttenbargen.

The remaining scenes take place in and around the inn. A crowd of excursionists, including Bolz, Frau Keferstein, Siebenmark, and Fräulein Isenbarn, fills the bar. They are waiting for the steamer "Primus" to take them back to the city. As they drink and converse, they hear Iver knocking on the floor above. Apparently he has not wounded himself severely.

The knocking draws attention away from the colorful action in the foreground. Fräulein Isenbarn responds to this call, or warning, from above, and as the play proceeds, she concerns herself more and more with Iver. Siebenmark, on the other hand, is at first interested only in his fiancée and his immediate business plans. He wants to get back to the city for an important appointment. She wants to stay and help Iver.

Both the surface and subsurface actions reach their critical point in a wild tavern scene (6) where the master of ceremonies is a man dressed as Frau Venus. Everyone is present, including Iver and Captain Pickenpack of the "Primus." The scene ends when Siebenmark recklessly decides to forfeit his financial future and stay at the inn with Fräulein Isenbarn until Monday. His reasons are obscure. Does he fear that he is going to lose his fiancée? Or does he feel obliged to help Iver?

At all events, Siebenmark is beginning to see things with different eyes and becomes more and more aware as the play continues. He tries to force Fräulein Isenbarn to make a decision about their relationship, saying, "We've got to come to a conclusion sometime." [21] But she repulses him with the reply, "But it will be simply an end and never a new beginning." He gives up and leaves to look after Iver, who is now walking about at night on the heath. When they meet, Siebenmark offers him money, in effect a bribe to get him away from Fräulein Isenbarn and also to salve his own conscience. But it is not quite as easy to evade responsibility or to avoid confronting one's own nature. Iver refuses the money and strikes back by demonstrating to Siebenmark how he is trapped in his own selfish ego.

Siebenmark is dismayed and maddened by this revelation about himself. In two scenes on the heath he rants and raves at his inability to overcome, and see beyond, his old nature. For him there is to be no dramatic end and new beginning. Iver, on the other hand, as if demonstrating one way of doing this, completes his suicide in scene 11. The events of the twelfth and final scene we have already recounted.

IV *Infinities of Time and Space*

The key to the understanding of Barlach's drama is clearly not to be found in the "concluding commentaries" but rather, as will be demonstrated, in the change in modes of temporal and spatial perception which takes place in the course of the action. The crucial issue for Barlach, at this time and throughout his career, is the problem of gaining perspective on two kinds of infinity. These are, temporarily speaking, total lack of time and eternity; and spatially speaking, the endless minutiae of this earth and limitless space. In *Der arme Vetter,* Iver has no time and feels overwhelmed by the things about him; and Fräulein Isenbarn hovers in the vastnesses of eternity and infinity. It is Siebenmark's task to try to assert himself as a human being against the two extremes. But first he must be shocked into real awareness.

Fräulein Isenbarn's concluding comments on end and beginning in scene 12 are the culmination of a series of remarks, more by others than herself, on time and time-consciousness. The issue is raised in scene 1 and immediately involves the concomitant themes of space and the relationship between surface and depth. The question raised is whether this is a particular Easter Sunday on the Elbe, an occasion to enjoy life, or Easter *sub specie aeternitatis,* the day of resurrection, not confined to a particular time or place.

When the play opens, Siebenmark speaks of this Easter as a "langweiliger Peter" ("dull Peter") and a thing of the past.[22] But Fräulein Isenbarn says she is going for a walk with Easter; she is still in the midst of the day. Thus she is irritated by Siebenmark's repeated reference to his watch. He keeps consulting it because he is preoccupied with the lateness of the hour and worried about making it to Lüttenbargen in time to catch the boat to the city. He has business to do there, and time is, for him, money.

Early in the scene, Iver, who has not yet put the bullet in his breast, comes rushing by. Siebenmark asks him for confirmation of the time and gets the obscure answer, "Yes, yes, high time." [23] They finally do agree on the precise time; it is 4:05. Siebenmark is relieved that the day has two more hours to live. Iver then asks directions to the inn at Lüttenbargen. Siebenmark obliges, but Iver rushes off in the wrong direction, saying, in answer to admonitions, that he cannot go along with them because he has no time; all ways are right, one must simply keep moving. Siebenmark lets him go, remarking, "He is in more of a rush than we."

This is only the beginning of the assault on Siebenmark's and the audience's naïve views of time and space. Heretofore his watch and his sense of direction have been his best defense in his struggle to give his life secure temporal and spatial limits. The difference in this regard between Siebenmark and Fräulein Isenbarn is brought out in the similes ("Gleichnisse") each has agreed to devise to describe the sound of water outside a ship's hull.[24] For Fräulein Isenbarn the hull is of no consequence; it is "like the moving and rushing of the blood in the veins of that greater life about us in which we float." Here, too, she is in the midst of things. But for Siebenmark the sound is "like the din of that unfathomable, eternally perverse absurdity in which we have to grope our way." In Siebenmark's simile the hull is all-important; it is like the walls he has constructed around his life to make it secure. "Thus I can illuminate my life like a room," he says, introducing the lantern motif, which assumes such importance as the play continues.

But listening to repetition of phrases and ideas such as "no time," "high time," and "he's in a hurry," which are sometimes intended seriously, sometimes in crude jest—"show him the way to the toilet, he's in a hurry" and once even in Low German dialect: "Ick hew keen Tid" ("I have no time")—confused by talk of directions like "northsouth" and "rightleft and leftright," Siebenmark loses his grasp on the rational co-ordinates of his "Lebensraum."[25] Thus, in the short scenes near the end, he moves in the dark aimlessly back and forth on the open heath along the river and talks about a new time-consciousness. He says, for example, to Customs Guard Sieg, "For a sleepy dormouse an hour can have a hundred years in its belly—I want to go on sleeping."[26] This is Siebenmark's moment of darkest despair, confusion, and disgust. And it is his closest approach to the moments of mystical illumination of which Iver and Fräulein Isenbarn speak.

Siebenmark never quite makes it up and over to that higher phase of existence, that state of ecstasy beyond the bounds of this world. His failure is complete when he takes hold of the lantern—the one that goes out in the next and final scene and the same metaphorical light he used to drive the shadows from his life-room—and examines the body of Iver, who has finally died of a hemorrhage. From this point on he may be a wiser man, but the earth has him again. He returns to the inn. His grotesque dance and blasphemous talk of resurrection in the last scene are not, however, just further evidence of the crudity and obtuseness he showed before. They are gestures of despair at having failed to see the true light and the mystical vision which other Barlach figures enjoy at comparable times. Siebenmark points to the dead Iver and says, "If he would only make his light glow, now is the time, but he has cloaked himself in darkness at the wrong time." [27]

Iver may have obscured his light at an inopportune time, but Siebenmark has at least the visual capacity to see that marriage to Fräulein Isenbarn under her conditions will be no marriage, for she is already dead. Casting a dark shadow of doubt over the validity of her alleged resurrection and new life, he says to her in his last important speech, "You have played a Valkyrie scene, bravo! You want to rise from this dead life to the higher death—Mrs. Siebenmark sacrifices herself to Siebenmark. She is letting herself be buried in Siebenmark in order to rise again in Iver. Those are merely hysterical fits. You have the choice between the two of us." [28] This speech is a fine example of how carefully and consistently Barlach makes it impossible for us to find final answers in even the most authoritative-sounding statements; for the audience must now have serious second thoughts regarding Fräulein Isenbarn's impressive speech about end and beginning. Indeed, on thinking back one recalls the peculiarly morbid eroticism in her attachment to Iver's corpse; and in retrospect her speeches do have the ring of hysteria.

Further doubts about Fräulein Isenbarn's role arise when one considers that she is only the third most important character. Granted, she is indispensable in the triangular situation; but in effect she is only the prize in the obscure, subsurface struggle between Iver and Siebenmark. She is an undramatic, rather passive figure; and, to judge by her speeches and actions in scene 1, she has already decided in favor of Iver. In fact, she seems scarcely to belong to this world. Her ecstatic choice of the "higher death" is simply the final, overt affirmation of the completed act, of the effortless, painless "resurrection," which she accomplishes with somnambular ease.

Iver, on the other hand, is situated at the opposite extreme. Whereas Fräulein Isenbarn stands outside time from the beginning, he is caught in it like a rat in a trap. He races frantically back and forth, a man with no time and for whom it is always high time. He is possessed by the most intense time-anxiety and agoraphobia. Like the doomed mouse in Franz Kafka's "Little Fable," he is engaged in a flight forward through the world, hoping to find the end simply by running on. Iver feels himself trapped while standing on the open heath. In scene 1 he points round about and says, "You know—I've lost my way, or I've been stuck into this hole here because of some stupidity." [29] By the hole—a synonym for "badly ventilated narrow pass" [30]—Iver means, of course, his disgusting, confining environment and, foremost, his own earthly self, his "Beschaffenheit," to use Barlach's word. He retches at the sight of others eating and drinking, for example, but the nausea is more acute when he accidentally looks at himself in the mirror while brushing his teeth. A man with a morbid sensitivity and conscience of cosmic proportions, he has no choice but to cut the Gordian knot and erase himself like a smudge from the pure face of eternity. [31]

Just before his death he stands in the dunes holding the ubiquitous lantern aloft so that it obscures the view of the stars and says, "It can't be denied, before my eyes this lantern is brighter than Sirius, an oil lamp outshines it. Everyone must simply see for himself how he can keep this selfish smudge pot from extinguishing all the celestial lights." [32] He sets the lamp down, crawls off into the bushes, and the flame goes out on the empty stage. This allegorizing tendency, seen here in the use of an eloquent object, is strong throughout the play, particularly in Iver's speeches. When he speaks of going home, of losing his way, or of his father, one must assume a double meaning. The abstract, or conceptual, element outweighs the concrete. In the end he himself becomes a ghostly abstraction.

Iver's end is a death and disfiguration, a grotesque parody on the mystery of Easter. Far from being the son, he is the "impoverished relation of a great lord." [33] That is, the family relationship is at best distant and obscure. His dying is simply the extinction of a "selfish smudge pot," a gloomy, hopeless event, an escape from the tyranny of his eyes with no compensating luminous vision. All he has seen throughout the play have been reflections of his own disgusting self.

Mirrors are important for Iver, and they are specified as properties in the sparse stage directions of two scenes.[34] Like the lamp, they are intended as eloquent, allegorical objects. Siebenmark, in conversation with customs guard Sieg, is the last to talk about mirrors. He says, "And now comes the craziest thing, even though others are really different from Siegs, you don't see anything but Siegs in the world—what can one do but run away, like a lap dog that barks into a mirror and a wolf howls back at him?" [35] Iver and Fräulein Isenbarn have thus finally made Siebenmark aware that the walls of his well-lit, secure life-room have been lined with mirrors and that he was not planning to marry his fiancée but rather himself in her.

In fact, if one looks for the basic structural principle of this play, it turns out to be one of repetitive and reflexive reference: in the vexing, horizontal mirror relationships between the characters, in the aimless shuttling back and forth from right to left and back again, in the repetition of the same ideas and phrases by various characters, and in the pronominal leitmotif "I-you-we-us." [36] Most of these reflections are thrown back in distorted form from the concave mirror of the grotesque, as when the wolf howls back at the lap dog, or the invisible "Chorus of Vengeance" in scene 6 reduces simple speeches to a string of nonsense syllables by repeating them in a crude musical setting.

Iver and Fräulein Isenbarn set themselves free, albeit in different ways, from this nightmarish funhouse or maze. Siebenmark is driven to the brink of suicide because he has absorbed Iver's horror of surface reality. Outwardly it is the discovery of Iver's corpse on the shore (scene 11) which saves him by distracting him from himself. He returns to his former condition despite his panic disgust with his bestial cur of a self. This is an obscure resolution, scarcely a victory. Yet it is the only significant one in the play. For it should now be clear that Siebenmark is Barlach's central and representative human character. He is the unifying focal point of the reflections.

V *Mirror and Crystal*

The figure of the mirror is distinctly symbolic of the human condition. It has far more content than Iver's abstractions. Siebenmark's path of initiation leads to the recognition of its true nature and his own. At first he is unaware that he is looking into mirrors and enjoys his unconscious narcissistic self-contemplation. After the climactic scene in the bar of the inn (scene 6), he finds that he has never seen, nor can ever see, anything but his own image. At this point the wolf howls back at the lap dog from the mirror, and the mirror has suddenly changed to an image of self-alienation. Siebenmark leaves the supposed security of the inn when it is brought home to him that he is living in a solipsistic world peopled by two-dimensional, intangible, dead Siebenmarks.

The unifying pattern of action in the whole play is that of Siebenmark's repeated attempts to break out of his world and his repeated frustration. Each time he tries to win Fräulein Isenbarn for his wife or bedfellow and to help Iver in the only way he knows how—by giving him money—he is rebuffed. The irony of the conclusion is that when Fräulein Isenbarn offers her earthly self to him, he understandably refuses. The conditions of the bargain offer no prospect of human contact. The new Siebenmark is not satisfied with earthly love alone.

Like other Barlach figures such as Squire Boll and Wau (*Der gestohlene Mond*), Siebenmark is at the outset a self-satisfied "Bürger" whose eyes are gradually opened to a new perspective on himself and the world. The following passage by a kindred protestant mystic, Jakob Böhme (1575–1624), describes aptly his situation at the end of the drama: "You have in your soul two eyes, they are set back to back; one looks into eternity, and the other looks back into nature and keeps moving in its own direction and seeks to satisfy its desires, and makes one mirror after the other: therefore let that one go, that's as it should be; God wants it that way." [37]

The play's greatest failing is that the supporting characters attract more attention than Siebenmark, and the dissatisfaction of many reviewers may be traced to the predominance given to the role of Iver. In *Der blaue Boll,* Barlach distributes the emphasis differently so that secondary figures like Grete Grüntal, who combines traits of Iver and Fräulein Isenbarn, are clearly subsidiary. Yet, in *Der arme Vetter* Siebenmark has as much right as Iver to be considered the title figure. The lines from which the title is taken—"In my misery as impoverished relation of a great lord"— apply in fact to Siebenmark.[38] He is the naïve central character, the Everyman of the allegorical tradition; and his two guides through the ordeal, his Virgil and Beatrice, are Iver and Fräulein Isenbarn. The parallel is not as farfetched as it might seem, for it is Fräulein Isenbarn who, to be sure without specific intent, points the way out of the slough of despond into which Iver has led him.

Her guidance is quite passive and unconscious. Her presence alone indicates to Siebenmark that one need not always look at things as Iver does, that the soul has another eye which can be trained on infinity. In scene 1 she tries to describe her Easter experience thus: "I feel, as I often have—but altogether differently today, as if there were in my soul a great confluence of things from many distances, as if something gleaming and mighty, that had been lost, is finding its way toward me again, as if something quite old and alien is becoming quite new and familiar again. Really, as if one were rising from the dead." [39]

The significant point here is that she is neither looking into a mirror nor up at the cold stars. She is not looking at all; she simply catches, like a prism or crystal, whatever it is that gleams and streams from afar. Free from tyranny of eyes focused on what Böhme calls nature, she has become a crystal to reflect and refract rays from the infinite. Thus she can mail the note saying "It's no longer me" and sign it with her full name, for she is blessed with that ideal orientation, "an orientation, whereby the ego remains conscious, that uncompleted operation which takes place when the ego becomes absorbed into essences without losing its own essence, transforms the world into itself, and transforms itself into the world . . ." [40] In other words, she is not exposed to the danger Seespeck sees in the contemplation of the stars, namely alienation from one's own vision and self.[41]

Iver, on the other hand, like Kule in *Der tote Tag,* is the slave of

his eyes and does suffer this estrangement. Just before his death
he turns from the "selfish smudge pot" of his earthly existence to
the cool magnificence of the limitless universe and is destroyed by
what Barlach elsewhere terms "the violent force of space perception." [42] His eyes have always been absorbing, drinking in sights
and light; in the author's terms, he lacks the capacity for refract-
ing and reflecting the drenching that comes from God's eyes. [43]
He is like the others who become ghosts in the fog around the inn
at Lüttenbargen.

What Siebenmark and the audience are supposed to realize is
that we need figures like Fräulein Isenbarn, "images, to which we
can cling with our souls, like telescopes, in whose lenses the rays
of infinity are gathered together. Only in the fact that they are
given to us, that they come near to us, that we let ourselves be
deceived by them—only in this does their grace and mercy consist." [44] Such images help bring together surface and infinity, time
and eternity, personality and un-personality, end and beginning. [45]

Barlach, the artist and moralist, pictures the ultimate human
values as sounds or rays of light issuing from somewhere in infinity. "They are manifestations of the universal soul," he writes,
"made known and audible in individual physicality and humanity.
Thus they provide the imperceptible with its peculiar kind of per-
ceptibility; they transfer some of their corporeality to the incor-
poreal and help it to find life in the light; they are, therefore, the
mirrors which capture the rays as they rush by so that they attract
my eyes' attention." [46] He then adds a counterbalancing statement which gives to the individual inherent values, color, and life
that enable him to assert himself against the infinite: "But now
isn't the mystery of this physicality and humanity equally great?
This act of mirroring the infinite, albeit in minute, most insignificant things? Everyone reflects back a small ray, doesn't he? And
toward them others reflect the infinite, and they absorb it and
weave it into something tangible and visible."

Fräulein Isenbarn belongs to the instruments in the first part of
this quotation. Only Siebenmark is receptive to the reflections of
others. He has normal vision, so to speak, and is spared "the violent force of space perception" which destroys Iver. For Siebenmark does not look toward the Gorgon's head of the infinite

absolute but rather at its reflection and refraction in "individual physicality and humanity."

From what has been shown so far, it should be clear that Barlach's *Der arme Vetter* is best explained in terms of perspective, and that to explain it on the basis of "concluding commentaries" and apparent self-interpretation is risky. As further evidence of this and as a contribution to the study of Barlach's artistic development, the following section will outline parallels between events of the play and the reorientation of his own vision.

VI "A Trip to the Steppes"

In the years prior to his epoch-making tour of Russia in 1906, Barlach worked with the false perspective of Iver and the unenlightened Siebenmark. That is, he was obsessed by Iver's temporal and spatial anxieties and, at the same time, like Siebenmark, devoted to the full foaming life. It was the Russian trip, he writes, that gave him his new way of looking at things: "A two months' trip to Russia in 1906 is probably what gave me the concept of limitlessness. . . . A limitlessness in which humanity could assert itself only as a crystallized, firmly formed configuration, if one wanted to hold on to humanity at all." [47]

The process of change can be shown by a glance at some of Barlach's early prose sketches. Until 1906 his muse was the "Witch of the Hours" ("Stundenhexe"), the title of a prose study written about 1895. His awe and terror at the passage of time emerge repeatedly in these early years. In their "flight from ominous questions about life" his thoughts race back and forth between past and future.[48] These thoughts also oscillate in a confusing way between the categories of time and space; in 1903 he wrote, "I look at space and fancy in merry moments that I behold time in person, God's housekeeper, standing there in the sky." [49] Also, his concept of crystallization betrays the same enthralment by time; a thin, toothless ex-convict, who managed to avoid death longer than his contemporaries, appears to Barlach for a moment as if he embodied a piece of life, "the shell of time, crystallized." [50] This is a far cry from Fräulein Isenbarn.

Before as well as after 1906, Barlach was occupied with the problem of how to bring earth and sky ("Himmel und die Welt")[51] into meaningful relationship, but he could not have

been further from the concepts of limitlessness and firm crystalline form than he is in a small landscape description of 1896–97
entitled "Around the Birches Weaves the Spring, and Even the
Elder Feels its Spell," a piece inspired by the vitalist philosophy of
the time and full of voluptuous *Jugendstil* motifs.[52] In it the
countryside is heavy, damp, almost soppy, and from it there is no
transition to the sky. Even chimney smoke, however much it may
yearn to rise, is rejected by the moist air and falls on the mead-
ows. The same may be said of the visual perspective; it has no
depth and never gets off the ground. The sky is lost from view as
attention is drawn to objects on the earth, all seen from close up.
Waddling, bowlegged geese pick at things; the path winds and
nestles "cozily" ("gemütlich") among the alders in the organic,
decorative style of those years. The reader is shown little nervous
buds on the branches and is finally asked to imagine the presence
of thousands of seeds under the ground, still asleep and dreaming
but harkening upward to live and blossom. Thus the landscape
dissolves to become an amorphous source of life.

The spell of the "Witch of the Hours" is broken for the first time
on Barlach's Russian tour as described in his "Russian Diary"
(1906 and after). She is replaced by a great cosmic clock whose
pendulum moves slowly from east to west with the sun.[53] In this
regard and in others, the trip results in a rebirth of feeling and a
new naïveté like that described by Fräulein Isenbarn.[54]

Yet at the outset the problem is far from solved. The danger of
losing oneself in the endless minutiae of the foreground, as happened to Iver and in the sketch on spring, still exists. Barlach is
well aware of this danger and states at the beginning the aim of
his observations in Russia. It is to bring foreground and background into relationship with each other. A representative occasion when the foreground vexatiously intrudes to obscure the
background—and thus the essential view—takes place on the
Vistula Bridge in Warsaw. Barlach writes: "If, for example, while
driving over the bridge our wagon had not collided with another
one, and if, as the two coachmen quarreled and the sounds whis-
tled about our ears like whiplashes, the grotesque silhouettes had
not been carved into the picture, then one could present a perfectly gently etched sheet showing the flat shore of a river moving
through endless lowlands." [55] The flat silhouettes of the grotesque

quarrel, comparable to some of Barlach's early two-dimensional drawings, effectively obscure the view into the limitless distance.

Later in the diary he turns his attention away from the grotesqueries and misery of folk life and focuses on the distance, though not on the sky. The distance as the distinct idea of infinity he finds to be the essence of all that is Russian in his experience.[56] What his eye learns to fix itself on are the sharp, firm lines of the hills on the horizon. The first time this happens in the diary, his glance follows the horizon to where it culminates in a mountain monastery. Continuing a long musical metaphor begun earlier, he writes of the monastery:

Bald and weighty, it detaches its contours as if from the profane past of charm and joy which has borne it up this far, by which it has been intensified and raised to the heights like a roof, which can then let all the heavens spread themselves out over it naturally and harmoniously. And with four towers and golden pinnacles its mood dies away [klingt aus]. As if pious instinct had built nests up there, fitted together like cellular tissue, as if the sacred joy of the landscape had suddenly been transformed from its upward striving into the triumph of fulfilment. A swarm of roofs, the monastery gleams in the sun and leaves the wretched start of its climb, the village at the foot of the beginning rise, far behind in obscure insignificance.[57]

Thus the landscape finds its fulfilment in the coming together of heaven and earth, in the monastery which partakes of both; for it is the transfiguration of what Barlach calls the hard crystal of the horizon.[58]

A few pages later a similar landscape, but lacking a cloister, is turned into a religious allegory as Barlach writes of "the figure of the steppe as soul." [59] Having found the crystallization point in the landscape, Barlach now translates the idea into human terms, putting the individual in the place of the monastery. The individual is the seeing man, the viewer. He stands, as it were, between the "process" of two infinities: Iver's chaotic earth and Fräulein Isenbarn's heavenly calm of eternity. The viewer, however, assumes a position analogous to Siebenmark's. He is aware of both infinities and finds himself, so to speak, at the junction of the two where, to repeat Barlach's words, under great pressure from both sides, humanity ("das Menschliche") can assert itself as firmly formed crystalline configuration.[60]

This conception of the human situation between heaven and earth clarifies somewhat the apparent confusion between the roles the devil and God play in Barlach's dramas and answers the question of how the grotesque satanic figure of Frau Venus in *Der arme Vetter* can justifiably call himself an "allerwertester Herrgottsvadder" (most esteemed Lord God Daddy). For Barlach writes (about 1914) in notes to a play called "The Day of Judgment" ("Der jüngste Tag") which he never completed: "The Devil becomes a god: for he makes man into a crystal of contradiction, of the igniting and intersection of two very different things, of struggle for struggle's sake, of fulfilment that ceases to be because it exists. *Devil and God are one. Therefore one is two*." [61] Thus though the two are one at the horizon point, so to speak, they must not be reconciled. In Barlach's formulation of the Faustian principle—that static fulfilment is death—dissonance is important, for harmony and unity make distinctions impossible and lead to morbid paralysis.

At the end of the notes to "The Last Judgment" we read: "Everything is one. But in order that it feel itself as one, it must be infinite. But if I am to feel, I must be able to make distinctions. If there is to be such a thing as All-One, then each and every thing must be different. God and devil must not become reconciled. Devil as depth, God as height, only depth and height together make a whole, etc."

Thus Barlach's concepts of horizon and crystallinity turn out to be a peculiarly human paradox, both fixed and in motion. In the landscape it is the apparently fixed but actually movable horizon. In his sculpture it is the rigid contour within which the lines express dynamic tension and motion. In *Der arme Vetter* it is the repetitive symmetry of repeated sally and rebuff, constant shifting from sensual to conceptual language and back again, the alternating stress on the two infinities of heaven and earth, beneath which, however, Siebenmark's ordeal proceeds with restless movement on a course of dialectical intensification.

The end of the drama is left open, and the movement, one suspects, continues like that of the great bird of prey described at the end of the Russian diary: "It is the storm's son, fatherly restlessness dwells in him, and his yearning, too, breeds in far distances. He searches and storms after it. But it keeps retreating before him, and the distance keeps feeding his fierce desire, and his soul swells with eternal yearning." [62]

Finally, the concept of crystallization and the conclusions about the trio of main figures in *Der arme Vetter* may be applied to the problem of where to place Barlach in the literary history of this century. For the sake of convenience he is usually classified as an Expressionist. Yet if, as Peter Szondi maintains, the Expressionists consciously view man as an abstraction, then Barlach must be considered apart and ahead of the movement.[63] The heroes of his best works—Siebenmark, old Sedemund, Squire Boll, Wau—are great because they preserve and intensify their distinct individuality. Barlach views man as firm crystalline configuration, as the crystal of the contradiction between his views of endless minutiae in the foreground and limitless space.

CHAPTER 3

Funny or Sad?

I N HIS *Essay on Comedy* (1877), George Meredith ventures
some generalizations on German national traits. "Nationally,
as well as individually," he writes, "when they are excited they are
in danger of the grotesque." In other words they lack the polish
and wit of the French, and "the discipline of the Comic Spirit is
needful to their growth." [1]

Barlach looks on the tradition of grotesque comedy—which is,
incidentally, quite as viable in France as it is in Germany—quite
differently. In 1895 he writes from Paris to his friend Friedrich
Düsel with naïve patriotic enthusiasm:

Hurrah for our victorious German spirit. What I am proud of is not our
cannons and fire-eating traits and our provincial countrymen but rather
our victorious German spirit. And, let me say, it is too stupid of us to
set up French art and French taste as models—too stupid. For we will
never match them. Many of our sculptors and painters imitate French
technique and succeed in being taken for Frenchmen at first glance—
truly beauty and charm are not our strength, our power; rather the opposite, ugliness, demonic passion, and grandiose grotesque originality,
and, above all, humor with its host of original figures. [2]

The letters and prose sketches of his later years give us the results of continued, maturer observation. In 1924 Barlach comments in a Christmas letter to Reinhard Piper; "German humor
rustles its pages in my ears with a wondrous sound, first it's Jean
Paul; then Kubin, as you rightly surmise, gives me pause . . ." [3]
To call Alfred Kubin (1877–1959) a humorist is to stretch the
concept mightily, but by doing so Barlach betrays his own predilection. For Kubin is best known for his eerie pen-and-ink illustra-
tions of horror stories and for one novel, *Die andere Seite* (1908).
This novel, with drawings by the author, consists of a series of

monstrous and disgusting nightmares which seem to give a pessimistic answer to the question posed in the autobiographical preface: "Are we then, I ask, no more than this framework of bones encased in hanks of flesh? Than this basket and sack filled with twitching, pumping, and sucking organs, like a nest full of naked sea-animals nestled together? Is this all?" [4]

Kubin's theme is moral and physical corruption; and he embellishes it with scenes of almost unimaginable bestiality and cannibalism. The novel ends with the dissolution of the whole city, its people and buildings. "Like a stream of lava, a mass of filth, garbage, blood, guts, animal and human cadavers moved slowly from the French Quarter." [5] Everyone ends as part of a "flood of carrion." And yet, Kubin writes, "these terrors and the humoristic strain in our life are closely connected." [6]

Barlach agrees with this and asserts twice in his letters that one of his more gruesome dramas, *Die Sündflut,* is full of humor.[7] However, he never matches Kubin's excesses and always shows us the other, sublime side which counterbalances the horror. He writes to Piper in 1923, "I have an instinctive, elemental desire to find the indication that there is a heaven above this slough; I would like to sense a reflection of eternal harmony above the terror. As in the case of Hogarth, where the essence of the picture is independent of the subject, where besides the cackle of scorn there is sonorous laughter." [8]

This paradoxical duality is the basis of Barlach's artistic vision. In 1911 he says in a letter, "Nature has solemnity and ease, grotesquery and humor in a single object and a single line. . . . I changed nothing of what I saw [namely, the fat beggar woman who served as subject for a sketch and a sculpture], I simply saw it that way because I saw the disgusting, the comical, and (I say this with all audacity) the divine at the same time." [9] And lastly, in a gloss on Dostoyevsky, he comments, "I know or intuit only this, something I know anyway: Sinners and the wretched are just as saintly as the saints themselves; there is no distinction, we are all accursed, exiled—convicts in this life . . ." [10]

To find further evidence that Barlach's humor is black and has a strong admixture of disgust one need only look at his graphic work. An early example is a ridiculous and repulsive drawing entitled "Liebespaar" ("Loving Couple").[11] It shows two fat, smirking, walrus-like human figures reclining on pillows (or rocks or shells?) that seem part of their bodies; the male fondles the female's breast while she gazes at him with dull expectancy. More forceful is the woodcut "Gott Bauch" ("God Belly") from the series *Die Wandlungen Gottes* (*The Transformations of God*)[12] With swinish face and an open mouth full of fangs, he bares his bloated belly displaying, in place of a navel, a second mouth with teeth. A smaller, rather silly figure holding a lyre celebrates his glory with a dance.

I Die echten Sedemunds

The play which best combines these graphic elements of comedy, disgust, and terror is *Die echten Sedemunds* (*The Genuine Sedemunds*), Barlach's third finished drama and only comedy. The central strand of action is an upheaval in the Sedemund family. Young Gerhard Sedemund returns to his home town when his father falsely reports that he is mortally ill. Actually, old Sedemund hopes to place his uncomfortably radical son in an insane asylum. His son learns of the ruse and takes the offensive. Before a large crowd gathered at the tomb of his mother, he forces his father to confess that he has in effect caused her suicide by forcing her into a false confession of infidelity. The elder Sedemund proceeds to confess all his sins quite openly and also to show that he had good human reasons for doing this to his frigid, self-righteous wife. By the end of the play he has proven himself more of a man than his son; and the latter—by now a sobered reformer—enters the asylum voluntarily. He does this out of contrition, so that the distressing disclosures may be blamed on his insanity and everything can return to normal.

As in any good comedy, the central action serves only as the barest framework to support a number of secondary actions and to provide good scenes for a crowd of colorful secondary characters. The drama unfolds amid the gay tumult of a small-town "Schützenfest"—a carnival and shooting match sponsored by the local rifle club. Thus it has that fulness and concreteness which, according to Jean Paul, comic presentation needs to fill the soul with sensuousness and to enflame it with that dithyramb which holds the world of the senses—comically distorted in its concave mirror—up against ideality.[13]

Also, of all of Barlach's plays, *Die echten Sedemunds* most closely resembles traditional comedy. It has many of the archaic ritualistic traits of Attic comedy described by F. M. Cornford.[14] It is full of personal invective and references to the human digestive and reproductive systems. It also has, near the conclusion, something like a marriage procession (*Kômos*), as well as a battle between a new and an old king (Sedemund junior and senior) and a nearly miraculous rejuvenation of the latter. The play ends with the prospect of a marriage between the father and a secondary female figure. Besides this we see the comical, or farcical, results of the false rumor that the lion has escaped from the menagerie; respected riflemen at the "Schützenfest" boast of their bravery but cannot hide their cowardice when they think the lion nearby.

There is comedy in the language as well. Uncle Waldemar cannot pronounce the letter *R,* and this makes his pompous way of talking even more ridiculous. Several characters speak in regional dialect, and one has a heavy Italian accent. And on one occasion the lion's name, Schesar, is changed through misunderstanding to Scheisser.[15] In general Barlach ridicules the weakness of the flesh. The play shows persons embarrassed by their instinct of fear or, in Bergson's words, "the soul *tantalised* by the needs of the body." [16]

However, Barlach's constitutional double vision—seeing solemnity and humor in a single line—determines the structure of the play. Accordingly, there is, in his concern with body and senses, something more unsettling than the distortion of Jean Paul's concave mirror. And our response to *Die echten Sedemunds* is more complicated than laughter at what Bergson calls a person embarrassed by the needs of the body. We find something disturbing and incongruous about several situations and characters. We see ordinary citizens become monsters and family relationships become perverted. We meet the unexpected at every turn. This small-town world becomes chaotic. The asylum inmate turns out to be sane. Respected civic figures go temporarily mad. All this is calculated to make the spectator lose his bearings and to shake him up. As Grude, on leave from the asylum, says, ". . . where fear won't educate them, an image will have to terrify them." [17]

At the heart of the main action lies the issue of fatherhood, or the relationship between parent and child. Old Sedemund wants to be rid of his son, but the latter suddenly forgets his filial piety and persecutes his father. The second unexpected reversal comes about when the old man is transformed into a vigorous, almost regal figure. Funeral Director Gierhahn wants to disown his illegitimate child and plans to pay a man named Schaukelstrick to admit paternity. Grude's wife is pregnant, but he at first shirks the responsibility of parenthood. The most ridiculous variation on this theme is the wretched tailor Mankmoos, who consoles himself with scrambled eggs while his hungry daughter looks on and his motherless children languish at home.

The motif of digestion and indigestion is the strongest and most striking in the play. Grude pronounces his world view in these terms: "True life is this: an eating process, a miracle of metamorphosis and digestion . . ." [18] The lion in the sideshow dies, quite unmetaphorically, of an intestinal ailment. Old Sedemund, supposedly sick, sits spread-legged in his bed enjoying a big breakfast, hears the news that Mrs. Mankmoos has just died, and laughs because she was so fat.

The death motif is thus also comic at times. Grude, for instance, spreads a false rumor that Gerhard Sedemund has died in order to get his father on his feet. Yet Mrs. Sedemund died slowly and painfully, and the threat of a lion on the loose inspires the townspeople with real fear for their lives.

The stage directions to the first scene prefigure the action of the entire drama. The audience looks directly at the outlandish, garish pictures decorating the carnival's menagerie. They are at once laughable in their "bloody romanticism" and terrifying because the largest and topmost one shows a lion apparently leaping from the heavens upon a few cocoa-colored men. [19] This painting combines, in a rude allegorical way, the comic, terrifying, and religious aspects of the play.

The first figure on stage is Sabine, a saintly, yet demonic and sensual girl in a wheelchair. And the dialogue begins, in stark contrast to the gay setting in the rifle club's garden, with the somber meeting of two apprentices. One of them carries a funeral wreath; the other carries a child's coffin but does not know where to deliver it. We learn immediately that hard by the new riflemen's clubhouse lies the old graveyard, and that a burial is to take place on this otherwise festive day. Later on, we see the two undertakers with the laughable names Gierhahn and Ehrbahn (rendered

Greedycock and Glorylane in Alex Page's translation), some pall-bearers, and a hearse driver, who suddenly and unaccountably cuts the ears off his horses.[20] These figures, while potentially comic, have a strikingly morbid aspect.

Nor are all the scenes laid in the rifle club's garden. The crucial one, the fifth, in which Gerhard Sedemund forces his father to confess his guilt, takes place before the ancestral tomb in the old churchyard. It begins with a bit of slapstick when Gierhahn and Ehrbahn think they have the lion cornered. However, the beast is already dead. Later the family dispute is punctuated by musical passages on a hurdy-gurdy. The total impression is such that, in answer to the question "How did you like it?" Sabine says, ". . . I'm sure I don't know whether it was funny or sad." [21]

The same comic-uncanny ambiguity characterizes the *Kômos*-like parade which the elder Sedemund leads from the Gothic chapel to the cemetery. It begins "half as carnival procession and half as funeral train." [22] Its members, a collection of townspeople, are "infernal roasts" and "infernal brethren" ("Höllenbraten" and "Höllenbrüder"), and they march to the strains of the hurdy-gurdy.[23] Finally the curtain falls on Mr. and Mrs. Grude as they dance "straight across the graves, right through the midst of the terror . . ." [24]

This is one important thing Barlach adds to the "humoristic sensuousness" suggested by Jean Paul: he keeps his audience aware of the dark side of sensuality, of death and decay. His characters are not simply embarrassed by the needs of their bodies; they also become uncomfortably conscious of the corrupt nature of the flesh. To judge by their figures of speech, they are obsessed by the stomach in particular, by eating, digesting, vomiting, and defecating. Grude maintains that all life is eating. And when Sedemund, Sr., sees the mangy pelt of the lion people had feared would devour them, he comes to the conclusion that "eating and being eaten seem in a way to be the same thing." [25] Even his rejuvenation is described as a digestive process: ". . . the lion is biting you. The good lion is transforming you as fodder inside him." [26]

The process, however, is not smooth. The diet of lion with its moral implications gives some people indigestion. Also, according to old Sedemund, even Christ would be unable to stomach knowledge of the former's family affairs. "He will vomit over us and befoul himself," he says, pointing to a statue of the Savior.[27] This foreshadows the answer to the question "What are the genuine Sedemunds?" Although the head of the family may have undergone a transformation, little has changed. Gerhard and the audience, however, have had their eyes opened. Young Sedemund sees himself, his family, and mankind as they really are. In his last speech he says, "Genuine Sedemund? Yes, that's the way they are, incorrigible! It stinks to high heaven with Sedemunds like a pile of garbage; a lion's mouth opens and howls rage over us and you call me a genuine Sedemund. At this moment any other name in the world is worthier than ours." [28] The name has indeed come into disrepute. But more important is the fact that the Sedemunds have, for a time at least, disregarded the opinion of the world and taken "the risk of ruthlessness." [29]

Of course not all the visceral talk is confined to religious metaphor. The second and third scenes of *Sedemunds* take place in the garden where much of the dialogue and action centers on food and drink. Barlach seems to find the bar or restaurant a suitable background for comic and grotesque scenes in many of his other works. *Der arme Vetter* (1918) has one where, to be sure, no lion is lurking in a graveyard nearby. Instead, a dense fog has closed around the inn at Lüttenbargen. A young man, who has shot himself in the chest, is the center of attention and ridicule. The tavern is full of people, and the stage directions call for "frenzied demands for food and drink." [30] The master of ceremonies has costumed himself grotesquely as Frau Venus and sits on a table surrounded by his mock court. His wit is predominantly scatological, but it ranges over the whole anatomy. He defends it and his drunkenness with the words, "My humor is no pussycat . . . I have to have something wet in my snout." [31]

One of his courtiers accommodates by blowing his nose and offers the handkerchief to Frau Venus saying, "Care to try mine?" The crowd's revulsion astonishes him, and he remarks, "I don't understand—it's the same kind of humor." He is wrong about this, for his is only one of several kinds of comedy here, not all of which contain such strong admixtures of disgust.

Repellent humor informs the entire scene. The effect is achieved through the wet handkerchief, by the grotesque dummy named "handsome Emil" and, in general, by stress on the flesh and its appetites. Barlach, it should be noted here, employs mannequins and wooden representations of the human figure in other plays too. Objects like Emil and the two life-sized wooden Turks in *Die echten Sedemunds* are at once comic and frightening.[32] The wooden Gothic crucifix in the latter play and the apostle in *Der blaue Boll* are at once awesome and strangely human. The handsome Emil as well as the two Christ figures are instrumental in the radical process Frau Venus calls the "disgust cure" ("Ekelkur") or "the beautiful-Emil-cure" ("die schöne Emilskur.").[33]

Cannibalism, too, can work such a cure. Hans Iver looks at the hungry crowd around him and says, "I have the impression that I'm among cannibals, just look how he bites me with his eyes, they're all eating a piece of me, they're swilling my blood—perhaps I will be a drop of good poison for them." [34] Cannibalism, metaphorical or actual, would seem to be the grotesque motif *par excellence*. Barlach often presents scenes of gluttony in order to revolt and, at times, amuse the observer, but his most immediately affecting passages are those that deal with the eating of human flesh.

In *Der tote Tag*, Mother cooks and serves up the allegorical horse. Religious and figurative allusions to cannibalism abound in *Der arme Vetter* and *Die echten Sedemunds* ("eating and being eaten"), but they are merely suggestive. However, the devouring of the Red Emperor in *Der Findling* (*The Foundling*, 1922) is quite real; the bloody remains are displayed on the stage. In all these cases, the motif reminds us of bestiality and arouses moral and physical revulsion. It excites what Wolfgang Michel calls "a panic terror of the body, a sensation which means in and of itself an abasement of the spirit." [35]

In *Der Findling*, Barlach further develops the theme of the disgust cure. But he goes to such extremes in his linguistic and stage devices that the play becomes turgid and quite obscure. It is his first and last attempt at writing dramatic verse. Certain passages are cast in free rhythm, others in rhymed doggerel, and the remainder in prose. The action is likewise a hodgepodge. And the overly abstract allegorical quality of it and the characters—more like some of his sculptures than living persons—accentuates the incoherence. The long alliterative passages are forced, and often he sacrifices clarity for the sake of sound.

Three years before his death Barlach mentions the play in a letter to Paul Schurek. He says that it was once his great hope, and he still feels affection for it. He recalls primarily the final episode, which describes the miraculous transfiguration of a scurvy, mangled, maggoty infant into a beautiful, shining child—a "Symbolum of the new time." [36] It was, however, his black cultural pessimism of the early 1920's that set the tone for the drama. In 1922, the year *Der Findling* appeared, he wrote of his fellow countrymen in a letter: "The people have gone to the dogs and have absolutely no inkling of the only possible meaning of life; one could despair that they are even capable of looking beyond their bare, gluttonous, greedy, avaricious self-righteousness, to sense that a goal is anything more than stomach-stuffing and intestinal contentment. You can talk all you want, an inner readiness must first be created through a radical softening of souls . . ." [37]

The play sets out to make our souls soft as butter with hammer blows like those of the stonemason, around whom the other figures gather. The first two—named simply Man and Woman—enter with the child. The weather is stormy, they are starving, and neither wants to carry the baby. Man refuses to take it from Woman and says, "Schab ab von dir deine Schäbigkeit, schmeiß hin den Schwamm deines Schadens, laß liegen das liebe Luder . . ." ("Shave off from you your shabbiness, fling forth the fungus of your disease, let the cute carrion croak . . .") [38] The strong shock comes from the perversion of human feeling in the parents and from the perversion of language for the sake of rather crude alliterative effects. The blasphemous parody of the Lord's Prayer, transforming it into a glutton's petition for satisfaction, and the crass variation of the sacrament of communion at the climax of the play work on the audience in the same way. And once again Barlach uses wooden figures on the stage, this time puppets.

The characters reach the nadir of degradation when they eat the cooked flesh of the Red Emperor. "Look how they sate themselves with disgust," says one of the two who don't partake of it. [39] This episode marks the new beginning, the start of the disgust cure. For when the stonemason reveals to them what they have eaten, these people recognize themselves for what they are: cannibals and wolves. They are then overcome by the desire to change, and the play turns increasingly metaphysical and mystical, so mystical that words can no longer describe what is taking place. A figure called Worshipper ("Beter") speaks: "No beginning, friend, and no end—it can't be done with words (taps his mouth)—it begins with silence. The tongue is the most superfluous thing, and what counts in the end—can't be said, it begins behind the tongue and behind words. (Howls.) It has passed, and I have to speak because I know nothing." [40]

It is in the mystical tradition when a speaker attains new heights of eloquence in preaching the inadequacy of words to describe the ineffable. However, in Barlach's case, it is not only paradoxical, but also grotesque. His manipulation of language, the heavy-handed alliteration, and the hyperboles distort, pervert and sometimes destroy the word in its accepted meaning. One thinks here of the character named Tenor. In his dismay over the revelation of his cannibalistic condition and in his desire to move beyond it he tries, starting with his fingers, to eat himself up. In the process he smears himself and several others with blood. [41]

Finally, at the very end, with the transfiguration of the mangy baby, the theme of cannibalism is brushed aside, and the play concludes on a lyric note. "Play" is perhaps the wrong designation, since this work is ill suited for the stage. To judge by its form, diction, and opaque structure it is rather an experiment. For Barlach's next drama, *Die Sündflut* (1924), bears strong similarities to it and yet earned him the recognition of the Kleist Prize.

II Seespeck

The opening chapter of Barlach's fragmentary autobiographical novel *Seespeck* (written 1913–14) depicts a grotesque episode that matches *Die echten Sedemunds* in literary quality. It mixes the three ingredients—comedy, fear, and disgust—in the proper proportions. It also shows us the beginning of Seespeck's disgust cure. Our laughter at it is compulsive and uncomfortable as when one laughs at deformity or insanity. The episode has sufficient stock comic elements but, partly because of the point of view, the finished product is anything but humorous. The reader is frightened and revolted.

The episode's frame is an evening trip by steamer from Buxtehude to Hamburg. Once on board, Seespeck descends to the ship's bar and meets the two persons who become opponents in a strange duel. The most striking one is Buur, the baker, a fat, slovenly man who commands everyone's attention. He has an inhuman, almost evil quality about him, for this obscene mountain of flesh is not in the least embarrassed by the needs of his body. Quite to the contrary, he flaunts his gluttony and his allegiance to God Belly. Although he has long since satisfied his appetite, he continues to consume beer and cookies soaked in it, befouling his front with the wet crumbs from his slobbering mouth. In the subterranean atmosphere of the bar, his audience grows, and he drinks and dunks with delight as if saying, "If you only knew what a loathsome thing I am." [42]

The baker is the incarnation of disgust. To make him even more terrible, he is unpredictable and always on the attack. His most telling weapons are self-degradation and total lack of shame. His actions reveal an extreme distortion and negation of human dignity, "revelations of imbecility, self-dismemberment, of the profanation and denial of everything sacred and of all that is humanly dignified, straight and whole. And the worst seemed to be that . . . this profanation was salted with boasting." [43] Yet for all the bragging, the baker's gestures are sometimes like those of a condemned man telling in pantomime of his pain and guilt.

But the baker is not the only one condemned. He has selected a victim, the blank-faced Hannis, a figure as grotesque as the baker but for altogether different reasons. Hannis' behavior is cool and his face as rigid as a mask except for the eyes, which are mobile and seem to absorb everything. At first he has nothing but scorn for his opponent; but the former's insatiable eyes undo him, and he becomes helpless, hypnotized by what revolts him. The baker seizes his advantage and degrades him (as Frau Venus degraded Iver) before the others, who occasionally find the spectacle repugnant. In his weakness, shame, and abject terror, Hannis seems to the onlooker Seespeck to be the personification of "Lebensangst" ("fear of life"), a man of fifty, who has shunned all strong emotional experience. [44] With his sensitivity and anxiety he is not only the perfect victim, but also the direct opposite of the baker.

Seespeck, too, is imprisoned here in the cabin by his own disgusted fascination; he has stayed on against his better judgment. Finally, he tries to rescue Hannis but finds himself suddenly face to face with the monster. On being subjected to the same degrading treatment, he makes a surprise attack and kicks the baker in the belly, "so that he made the fat monstrosity painfully aware of his corporeality." [45] This unreasoned act corresponds to what Barlach tries to accomplish elsewhere, namely, to make the reader or spectator painfully aware of his corporeal nature with hammer-like blows.

Like the kick, most of the action in the episode is sudden and unexpected, and the effect is unsettling. All the events are seen through Seespeck's eyes, and we learn nothing beyond his immediate thoughts and sensations. As he becomes enthralled by the disgusting spectacle, so does the reader. To make matters worse, his vision is disturbed by a hangover, so that even before he meets the baker, the process of alienation and disruption has begun. His perceptions are so disordered "that he felt as if he were standing without a handhold on a high ladder or as if he were seized by an attack of dizziness, because he was gazing into a mirror in which everything that normally lay calm and stood still was moving." [46]

Jean Paul's concave mirror is but a mild caricature of the world of the senses. Its grotesque counterpart, Seespeck's mirror, reflects a world in dissolution and affects him with vertigo and nausea, which are aggravated by the ship's rocking and the threat of the baker to the point of extreme disgust and "panic terror of the body." Also, because of his excesses the night before, Seespeck suffers, like Hannis, from hypersensitivity, so that things become magnified far out of proportion. The awareness that his tie keeps slipping down distresses him painfully; when the baker sticks out his tongue and Hannis responds with a stare, we have no childish situation but rather a deadly duel.

All this makes the effect of the scene grotesque rather than comic, for with a change of perspective the baker might well have been a clown rather than a monster. Comedy, says Bergson repeatedly, must not arouse our feelings; but in the first chapter of *Seespeck*, as elsewhere in Barlach's writings, the aim is precisely to arouse the reader's feelings. The crowds in Barlach's barrooms may be able to laugh in detachment at the spectacle of the baker or Frau Venus, but the reader is made to feel discomfort. To excite this feeling Barlach lets loose, in long periods, a flood of words like "hideousness," "filth," "suffocate," "throttle," "stinking pustules from the quagmire," "malignant," and "sinister," until the episode

comes to an arbitrary end with the boat's docking. Yet even with
the tension eased, the narrator adds another image of distortion:
as the baker walks off, "his shadow aped his walk and exaggerated
everything in breadth and bulk." [47] This is, however, only a weak
reverberation of what has gone before. In spewing forth his disgust
in hyperboles piled one on another, Barlach seems to have exhausted the powers of exaggeration in himself and in the language.

Barlach employs language and sound for grotesque purposes,
just as he does with other components of style. In later works
he uses words more skilfully than in *Seespeck*. Certain phrases,
words, and sounds are stressed, repeated, and piled up, as are the
impressions of the baker, to give the language a cumulative op-
pressive force. This is not Bergson's comic, Jack-in-the-box kind of
repetition where words are repressed and repeatedly spring up
anew.[48]

It is rather an insistent pounding repetition. Like the hard stress
in the frequent alliterative passages of Barlach's plays, it disturbs
rather than delights with its rude forcing of language and syntax.
The constant accentuation of little words like "belly" and "glut"
seems at first to give them real substance. But in the end they
suffer the same semantic exhaustion as do repeated abstractions
like "dignity" and "righteousness."

The grotesque extremes of sensuality (baker Buur) and spiritual abstraction (Hannis) thus lie behind Barlach's treatment of
language. The recurrent stress on the sensuous element, or meat,
of certain words finally makes them sound absurd, as when the
Chorus of Vengeance in *Der arme Vetter* picks up the phrase
"Geh du—ich nicht" ("You go—I won't") and turns it into a string
of nonsense syllables by singing to the tune of the drinking song
"Krambambuli": "Geduichnicht—gedaichnicht—gedaichnicht—
gedu—geda—geda—ich nicht." [49] This is an extreme example of
what happens repeatedly in this play (for instance the toying with
the pronouns "I—you—we—us") and in *Die echten Sedemunds*
where the words "Ich auch" ("Me too") are repeated over and
over again until they become ridiculous. On the other hand, repetition of abstract words from the moral sphere with varying, often
contradictory connotations renders them equally meaningless.

III "*Grotesque*" *as an Esthetic Term*

The grotesque differs from the comic in that it introduces incongruous elements from beyond the bounds of humor. Lee B. Jennings reduces these to the common denominator of fear.[50] Yet a close look at the grotesque literature of the modern period suggests that disgust and the demonic also deserve inclusion. Since the end of the nineteenth century, an ugly, perverse, anti-poetic force has intruded, mainly in the form of obsessive emphasis on the organs and biological functions of the body. This concern may take the shape of reveling in bestiality or of an ascetic, fanatic purity. We find both extremes in Barlach.

In its effect on the observer, the grotesque generally arouses an emotional response of laughter and fear or disgust. It has an immediate, primitive effect, whereas good comedy is civilized, creates esthetic distance, is objective and public rather than subjective and personal. In fact, as we have noted in *Seespeck*, the threatening immediacy of the grotesque baker—in himself both ridiculous and fearsome—is so great that we are scarcely amused. In this regard Kenneth Burke goes so far as to say, "Humor specializes in incongruities; but by its trick of 'conversion downwards,' by its stylistic ways for reassuring us in dwarfing the magnitude of obstacles or threats, it provides us relief in laughter. The grotesque is the cult of incongruity *without* laughter. . . . Insofar as you are in sympathy with it, it is in deadly earnest." [51] Seespeck and the reader who is drawn to sympathize with him are subjected to unrelieved humiliation, whereas in comedy the object is humiliated.

Baker Buur is the grotesque object *par excellence*. A comic writer would tone down his slovenly enormity, endow him with a mechanical rigidity, and provide him with no more ugliness than a normal person could imitate. His deformity would seem a mask, at most hinting at the demon behind it. The grotesque writer, on the other hand, presents a monster and exaggerates its inhuman abnormality. Mask and essence seem to merge, thus making the grotesque figure stronger and more dangerous than the comic one with its dual nature. Baker Buur's soul is not tantalized by the needs of his body. He has no soul and is consequently somewhat like Bergson's life principle gone wild. He moves, even dances with no trace of mechanical rigidity. As the embodiment of flesh and appetite, he tantalizes others. In fact, he fascinates poor Hannis and paralyzes him with horror and disgust. Nor can the ascetic Hannis be considered comic. He is simply the wretched victim.

Jennings maintains that the grotesque is primarily a visual phenomenon.[52] But we have seen how the treatment of body and flesh finds its analogy in the use and misuse of words in these plays. Barlach adheres to the "cult of incongruity" to which Kenneth Burke refers. The grotesque object itself does not display any marked split, but in Barlach's poetic world things are constantly at odds with one another: heaven and hell, saints and sinners, carnivals and funerals. And the typical Barlach hero is at odds with himself. We have seen the extreme exaggeration of this in *Der Findling*, where Tenor tries to devour himself in order to make way for his new and better self. Similarly, Siebenmark rages against himself in the mad scenes of *Der arme Vetter;* and the motif echoes through *Die echten Sedemunds* in statements like "everyone is a Doppelgänger" or "Herr Sedemund is a porter for his own self." [53] This conflict between two identities under the same name is coupled with the urge for self-destruction.

Of the grotesque situation Jennings writes, ". . . the threat of chaos brings with it a terrifying vertigo, but the footing is regained as we attain the superior vantage point of the observer." [54] The audience loses its bearings when it sees the "violation of the basic norms of experience prevailing in our daily life." The perversion of family relationships in *Die echten Sedemunds* and the confusion in conceptions of time and space in *Der arme Vetter* will serve as two examples of many that could be culled from the plays and novels.

For all this, the atmosphere of Barlach's work is not one of unrelieved disgust and ascetic denial of the flesh. The observer does eventually gain a superior vantage point from which he can view with hope the prospect of reconciliation. Nor are these works cynical about language as is, say, Eugène Ionesco's *Bald Soprano*. They have a religious warmth and make a paradoxical statement of faith. Granting, for instance, that words are worthless for knowing in the ordinary sense, Barlach nevertheless believes that they have an unlimited potential and that to use them properly is something like an act of reverence. In 1932 he wrote to Pastor

Zimmermann: "You see, people want to 'know' and demand the word, but words are useless, at best a crutch for those who are content to hobble. And yet there is something in words that penetrates to the inmost essence when they come from purity and absolute truth. . . . These verbal trifles can even border on the absolute—quantity, tone, pure form are the keepers of mysteries . . ." [55]

The ideas expressed here, and even certain phrases like "from purity" ("aus dem Lautersten"), read like the writings of the old German mystics, Meister Eckhart in particular. They, too, despaired of the power of words and used language as a weapon against itself, at the same time actually opening up new creative linguistic possibilities. Like Barlach they employed such devices as paradox, antithetical parallelism, hyperbole, and repetition. Their style, like Barlach's, was primarily nominal. They enriched the German vocabulary with abstract nouns in "-heit" and "-keit," and they substantivized infinitives.

Similarly, Barlach's works do more than show us the grotesque extremes of sensuality and "Lebensangst." Characters at opposite ends of the scale—the baker and Hannis, Frau Venus and Iver, to mention two of several pairs—are caught in this lower phase of existence, this badly ventilated narrow pass. But they are usually foils for thoughtful sensualists like Seespeck and Siebenmark who are ready to risk transformation and become something better. Because they are aware of the grotesque dissonances in themselves and this world, and because they do not run away, they learn to see rightly. They have appetites, but they are not gluttons, nor are they afraid of being eaten. These central figures are strong and have a sense of humor. Their vision acquires distance.

In narrative and drama Barlach works to achieve the ends which Paul Fechter descries in his graphic and plastic work: ". . . his ever recurrent struggle with the spirit of gravity, his attempt insofar to overcome it that he succeeds, at least figuratively, in freeing man from the earth and bringing him to a state of hovering and rising out of the chthonic realm into a purer one." [56] And he accomplishes this through the grotesque, which is, in Friedrich Dürrenmatt's words, "a sensual paradox, the form given to formlessness, the face of a faceless world." [57]

Baudelaire points to the same paradox when he says that,

whereas laughter caused by comedy is the expression of man's superiority over man, laughter caused by the grotesque is the expression of man's superiority over nature.[58] Its comic and demonic elements not only arouse fear and disgust, they also, in the end, purge the soul and open the eyes. The effect of the grotesque is in fact what Frau Venus calls an "Ekelkur"—a cure worked by disgust.

CHAPTER 4

Diction in Die Sündflut: *Prattling about God*

IN 1924, Barlach received the Kleist Prize—a significant award which was made each year in Germany to encourage dramatic talent—for *Die Sündflut* and appreciated the recognition despite the fact that he was no longer a beginner. Since then, the play has undergone much critical discussion, some of it quite negative.[1] Most treatments acknowledge its excellence without, however, demonstrating why it is good. They are generally content with plot summaries and comments on its religious and philosophical ideas. Actually the theological concepts, and the theodicy question in particular, have only secondary significance. They are a means, not an end.

During his lifetime, Barlach had sufficient occasion to complain of misunderstanding and misinterpretation. Before a premiere performance in 1925 he sent his brother Hans the two tickets which had been destined for his own use. The accompanying letter shows a peculiar mixture of indifference and concern over the drama's destinies:

I am going to stay here [in Güstrow] in the company of my resignation. *Never* have I been so sure of what I was doing, which of course will not keep the misunderstanding from being enormous. From reviews of other performances I see that it is not easy to recognize that a physical and superficial annihilation can be an inward triumph and that the man who is blessed and saved need not be the greatest. But enough of this, I'd rather say no more about the platitude that good and evil are simply relative concepts. If you don't expect too much, you might even have a salutary evening; one just looks on and sits high and dry when the waters come.[2]

I *Dialogue as Action*

Barlach's fears proved justified. The theaters and the reading public missed the point. "Already the pastors and their ladies' groups are reading my *Sündflut* with assigned roles. And I had nothing up my sleeve but to demonstrate that the old fable is simply absurd." [3] As anyone can see on close examination, the play should have struck these readers as blasphemous.

It contains certain elements from the sixth chapter of Genesis: Noah and his family, one of the "mighty men," and the Lord's grief at the wickedness of mankind. The remainder is Barlach's invention. He places one mighty man (named Calan) beside Noah and constructs his play in the form of a dialogue, not a conflict, between the two. They are not really enemies. Calan, in fact, helps Noah defend himself and recover his property, and he provides Noah's sons with wives.

To be sure, the dialogue is not entirely verbal. Calan sometimes illustrates his arguments by bloody deeds with the sword. Yet all these actions aim to prove something about the connections between man and his god and between men. The discussion covers such topics as the nature of the divine, the problem of evil, man's attitude toward his god, family relationships, and the relationship between master and servant.

These abstractions appear on stage in concrete form and vivid costume. A hunchbacked leper introduces Parts I and II with bitter comments on the god that made him this way. The Lord appears in two guises. In Part I he enters dressed as an aristocratic traveler; in other words, as Calan sees him. In Parts II and III he takes the shape of a crippled beggar. This is Noah's god. When Noah meets the aristocratic traveler in Part IV, it is a reflection of a theological confusion in his mind which results from his debates with Calan.

In a letter with specific reference to *Die Sündflut*, Barlach defends this seemingly blasphemous polytheism as follows:

All speaking about "god" is working with an inappropriate tool, the rationally ordered word. It can only help to give approximate expression to what one feels in so far as it is humanly comprehensible. Beyond this point, man may believe his intuition; but, on the other hand, he possesses only human means for formulating the content of that faith. God is (thank God) quite certainly no man; men will never know God; their ultimate pronouncement will always give only an image of idealized humanity. Thus we have as many gods as there are god-seekers.[4]

Noah is confused because he has undergone severe trials. Firstly, his wife, his sons, and their wives have robbed him of his pious calm. Through a kind of religious blackmail they repeatedly force him to accede to their godless desires. Secondly, Calan has shaken his faith by argument and by a shocking experiment. He orders his servant to cut the hands off an innocent young shepherd and challenges Noah's god—and Noah as well—to prove his goodness by preventing it. Both fail, and Noah does nothing but cover his ears to shut out the screams. Calan then nails the hands to a post as a constant visual reminder.

Noah's god gets his vengeance at the last. The waters are rising, and Calan lies on the ground tied hand and foot to the leper. The last man on earth left alive turns out to be the handless herdsman, and he, of course, cannot untie them. Yet this god's triumph is a hollow one, and Calan has only scorn for it. He is about to experience mystical union with his true god who has no need for such petty proofs of his power.

The dialogue between Noah and Calan concludes in the final speeches. Noah still uses the old vocabulary of the Lord as his shepherd and as the immutable god of vengeance. Calan retorts, "That is the god of floods and flesh, that is the god of whom it is said: the world is tinier than nothing and god is all. But I see the other god of whom it shall be said: the world is great and god is tinier than nothing—a point, a glimmer, and everything begins in him and everything ceases in him. He is without shape or voice."[5] These words articulate the radical change that has been latent in Calan since the opening scene. His impious sadism must be viewed as evidence that he has already rejected simple answers and is taking the risk of ruthlessness in his search for the true god.

At the last, Noah boards his ark which carries two animals of every sort. It also carries a collection of human beings whose natures insure that the world will be no better or worse after the flood.

Theater audiences and directors proved as incapable of grappling with the play as were the ministers and ladies. Barlach complains, ". . . the people feel insulted by such demands on their thinking capacity, and moreover, what devil rides those theater directors causing them to make oratorios and Mysteries out of my dramas instead of entertaining pieces!" [6] Steeped in the expressionistic dramaturgy of the 1920's, they produced *The Flood* and his other plays in an inappropriate stylization. "Film tempo and expression, I want nothing to do with it," he writes in 1920 of the staging of *Die echten Sedemunds*, ". . . and the basic tone of the whole thing—screaming and monumental style-buffoonery." [7]

II *Verbalization and Verbosity*

Barlach's language, like his plays, is admittedly highly stylized, but not in the direction of extravagance, as the theatrical people seemed to assume. He aimed rather at rough simplicity. His characters may sometimes speak in grandiose phrases, but the intent is to expose these as windy words. Consequently Barlach was an outsider among his expressionist contemporaries and exposed to misunderstanding precisely because of his straightforwardness. Otto Mann calls him "linguistically the most powerful" writer of the time, because his diction is so remote from intellectual stylization.[8] Mann has other illuminating things to say on the subject but then drops it to comment at length on the dramatist's dangerous tendency to play the prophet and preach the Barlachian way to redemption. Among other critics, Hans Schwerte and Elisabeth Lichter have recognized the importance of Barlach's language and have opened the way for further work in this direction.[9]

In his postscript to the collected dramas, Klaus Lazarowicz does no more than discuss Barlach's symbolism in broad terms. He passes quickly over the issue of diction by remarking on Barlach's mistrust of the word and saying that "the poet strives to move beyond words to images." [10] This position is misleading if taken at face value, for it presents only half the picture. And one must recognize, as do Schwerte and Mann, that words and their sounds constitute the fiber of Barlach's literary work.

The question is still open as to what relevance Barlach's linguistic power has in the totality of any one drama. If—and this seems unlikely—he is striving to overcome language or just to propagate a new way to redemption, why would he take such pains in composition as he describes in the following passage from a letter: "I often struggle for days with a single word, turn a sentence with three words endlessly this way and that, and often have to give up because I can't find a word with the right number of syllables; the word doesn't exist, but it should exist. The opinion, the thought, the event in themselves are completely worthless." [11]

Die Sündflut is well suited for analysis on the basis of diction because it is at least as good as any other play by Barlach and far better than *Der Findling*. Even though they share many characteristics such as alliteration, mythical background, and mystical experience, *Die Sündflut* succeeds where the earlier play failed. The following reflections on simplicity in language tell us why. They appear in a letter dated 1924, the year Barlach completed *Die Sündflut*. "The unheard-of can only be described with unheard-of words; but unheard-of words suddenly become false words; for the obvious, which is inherent in the unheard-of and which I want to show so that the result will satisfy and will *have to* be accepted, the obvious depends on the plainest word; the problem is: to be forceful without seeming forced." [12]

Die Sündflut, by comparison, does not seem forced. Yet it does show Barlach's compelling linguistic virtuosity, and the spoken word is one of its central issues. In fact, the essence of the whole drama and of Barlach's world view can best be extracted from observation of the language of this play. The striking use of alliteration, repetition, parallelism, and the plays on words clearly have more than decorative function.

Otto Mann suggests that alliteration is a "style principle" in Barlach's plays, but he neglects to draw the consequences of this statement.[13] Alliteration is indeed important, and it is used in quite appropriate ways. For example, it gives a remarkably expressive vigor to Calan's speech to the Beggar-Lord after he has had the shepherd's hands cut off in order to put Noah and his god to the test. "Aber die Hände habe ich abgeschlagen und annageln lassen—ich, Calan, ein Kind des Gottes, der mir die Kraft gegeben hat, kein Knecht zu sein." (But I have had the hands cut off and nailed up—I, Calan, a child of the god who gave me the strength not to be a servant.)[14] These are plain words, quite unlike those quoted from *Der Findling* in the previous chapter; and this is one reason for their forcefulness.

More specifically, we should note that the first part of the passage, up to the dash, is held together by the *a* assonance and alliteration but is itself split rhythmically in two by the *ich*. Because of the alliteration, the first part must be read with heavy stress on the initial syllables. The *ich* then receives redoubled emphasis since it is totally isolated and, in its position just before another accented syllable, must be made to stand out. The *ich*, obviously the key word now, is repeated at the beginning of the second unit with the same emphasis for the same reasons. The effect of the second unit is one of dynamic, explosive emphasis with the rapid-fire repetition of initial consonants *k* and *g*, which re-echo in the same words throughout the play. The speech itself reinforces our impression of the action and is fully consonant with Calan's violent, aggressive nature.

Not self-assertion, but the sound of sudden disaster is suggested in the following speech by the servant Chus, as he tells how the Beggar-Lord has dispersed Calan's herds: "Ein zorniger Flug großer Hornisse stieß auf die Kamele, stürzte ihnen Stiche über Nüstern und Augen, über Beine und Bäuche, bohrte ihnen Gift in Ohren und After . . ." (An angry swarm of big hornets fell upon the camels, stabbed stings over nostrils and eyes, over legs and bellies, bored poison into ears and hind quarters . . .).[15] The alliterative pattern of *s, st, b,* and *o* and *a* vowels accentuates the choppy rhythm. The formulary character of the short word groups with two strong, often alliterative, accented syllables is reminiscent of the primitive Old High German incantation.

Barlach also uses sound to recapture the ecstasy of an overpowering emotional experience. Awah, the beautiful pagan girl over whom Noah's sons quarrel and whose intuitive perceptions of the divine Noah envies, begins a speech with: "Ich sehe, wie es klingt, ich höre, wie es schwingt, das Ende wiegt den Anfang in den Armen." (I see how it rings, I hear how it swings, the end rocks the beginning in its arms.)[16] The whole passage echoes the rocking of the flood waves: ". . . es spielen Wort und Welle" (. . . word and wave are playing). Although it is constructed on much the same pattern of Chus's speech, it gets its singsong, cyclical quality from a lengthening of the word groups by adjectives and from the use of end rhyme.

On the other hand, similar means may be used to describe a terrifying experience like that of Noah's son Japhet when the angels fly by "im Gewand wie fließendes Geflecht von Sonnenstrahlen, zwei redende Riesen mit Gerinne und Gehetz und Gekeuch und Gehusch von Flügeln aus Luft hinter sich an den Fersen" (. . . in raiment like a flowing mesh of sunbeams, two talking giants with a racing and chasing and panting and hurrying of wings made of air behind them at their heels).[17] These are not playful words but hard ones which must be read with uninterrupted, breathless haste. They are intended to reproduce the original force which was so strong that Japhet says, "I was ground between their words as if by millstones."

No less expressive in its explosive rage and disgust is the leper's venomous attack on the Lord with its two long strings of alliterative words closed off by the vicious sounds of *Krallen* and *kratzen:* "Glaubst du, daß er ein einziges Mal mit Essen überschlägt, weil all das menschliche Elend mit seinem Brand und seiner Bitterkeit in seinem behäbigen Bauch beißt und die Krallen der Gebete seinen Magen wund kratzen?" (Do you think that he ever skips a single meal because all human misery with its burning and its bitterness is biting in his fat stomach, and the claws of prayers scratch his belly bloody?)[18]

It should be noted here that, though these speeches are well calculated to fit the situation, the words and sounds have an existence independent of the speakers. Awah and Japhet display an unrealistic eloquence considering their emotional states and the unexceptional quality of their minds. Also, Noah's speeches are often larded with l sounds as in the phrase ". . . als ob die Fettigkeit des Landes in linder leiser Lust zerflösse" (as if the fatness of the land were dissolving in soft gentle joy).[19] Yet when he gives an order for meat to be brought to the Beggar-Lord and demands "des Lammes leckerstes Lendenstück" (the lamb's most luscious loin piece), Calan interrupts and, using the same letter with longer, darker vowels, completes the sentence on an ugly note: ". . . für einen alten Lügner und Lumpen, der längst im Grabe faulen müßte" (. . . for an old liar and scoundrel who should long ago have been rotting in his grave).[20]

III *Semantic Exhaustion*

Verbal and phonic devices serve not only to reinforce meaning and mood; they also determine the structure and reveal the tension of the drama as a whole. Certain formulary, alliterative phrases like leitmotifs with variations and spoken by various characters reverberate through the whole drama. Thus Barlach plays on the phonic memory of the listener and on the large scale of associations which these words and sounds eventually evoke. Such a formula is *Freude, Friede, Freiheit* (felicity, friendliness—or peace—freedom). It is originally and basically part of Noah's vocabulary. He uses it twice in Part II, Scene 2 after the angels have visited his camp and he has missed seeing them. Noah moans and blames his sons for his own failure: "[Ich] ließ mich von euren blasigen Worten umwinden und von euren harzigen Händen halten—und so gingen Freude, Friede, Freiheit." (I let myself be entwined by your windy words and be restrained by your pitchy paws—and so felicity, friendliness, freedom are gone.)[21] Noah's whole life seems to hang on the prospect of, or longing for, these three abstractions; but he never finds them. They prove to be chimerical ideals which eventually rot and crumble under the repeated assault of Calan's, or Barlach's, "inquiring and investigating" (*Fragen und Forschen*).[22]

To tighten the association, Noah repeats the words a third time out of mistaken pity for Calan, referring to the triad in the singular: "Poor, terrible Calan, where is friendliness, felicity, freedom to be found for you?"[23] Calan indicates that the phrase means little to him, and by the end of the play the words are emptied of their original meaning for the audience as well. The process begins when they are linked by alliteration with "Fettigkeit" (fatness), "fürchten" (to fear), and "Fleisch und Verderben" (two words from Genesis meaning flesh and corruption or destruction).[24]

Flesh and corruption in the person of the depraved pagan girl called "fat Zebid" constitute at first in Noah's eyes a threat to his pious peace. Yet within a short time he finds himself defending her before the Lord for the sake of peace and joy: "Kann sie dafür, daß ihre Speise Fraß war und feistes Verderben ansetzte?" (Can she help it if her food was fodder and fattened her with corpulent corruption?)[25] To keep peace in the family at all costs, Noah is traveling against the Lord's will to fetch this epitome of depravity into his household and on board the ark. He is aware of the dangerous ambiguity and vagueness in his *Friede, Freude, Freiheit,* but his weak acquiescence to his sons' wishes indicates what little content the words have. In practice the one seems to cancel out the other. He has to sacrifice joy and freedom to pursue an ever elusive peace.

It is significant that the cross-eyed, lascivious Japhet is the last to mouth the phrase—this time in adjective form: "frei, froh und friedlich"—and that he directs it to Zebid, with the result that *Friede, Freude, Freiheit* become entwined not only with *Fraß* and *feistes Verderben* but also with the object of Japhet's longing: "eine Frau mit festem Fleisch" (a woman with firm flesh) and the whole crude sensuality of Japhet and Zebid.[26] Noah's concept of freedom, "die ganze schöne Freiheit" (all that nice freedom), is also laid bare in its shallowness by Ham, who thinks of it as license to dominate the earth.

This long development may be seen in miniature in Part II where the loss of verbal meaning, along with the collapse of proper family relationships, is shown primarily through plays on words. As usual, Noah's sons are concerned with the problem presented by their sexual urges. Noah begins: "Es bekümmert mich, daß ihr unzufrieden seid" (It grieves me that you are discontented), whereupon Sem and Japhet gloss the speech as if their father were no longer present. Sem: "Ei ja, es bekümmert ihn . . . Er will gottgefällige Töchter, als ob es nicht vielmehr darauf ankäme, was für Frauen wir haben wollten." (Oh yes, it grieves him . . . He wants daughters pleasing to God, as if it were not more important to consider what kind of wives we want.) And then Japhet: "Mich bekümmert sein Kummer, aber darum sollen unsere Kinder nicht kümmerlich geraten. Ich will eine Frau mit festem Fleisch . . . gottgefällig, nein, gottgefällig sind sie nicht, die da auf der anderen Flußseite, aber mir genügt es, daß sie mir gefallen" (His grief grieves me, but our children should not turn out miserably on that account. I want a woman with firm flesh

. . . pleasing to God, no, that they are not, those women on the other side of the river, but it's enough for me that they please me).[27]

Noah's piety and fatherly concern suffer two blows in these monologic speeches, one from his sons' scorn and the other from their toying with his words which opens them to question as to their essential and experiential meaning. Even Japhet's sincerity is doubtful when he talks about children. They are at best secondary to the pleasures of a certain kind of wife.

Barlach's penetrating assault on words can also lead in the direction of clarity as in the instance of the words *Herr, Knecht, Vater, Sohn,* and *Kind* (lord, servant, father, son, and child). In fact, the structure of *Die Sündflut* is reflected best in the interplay of the words and concepts dealing with relationships between lord and servant, father and son. The development begins in the opening scene when the angel speaks to the Lord and refers to Noah as "dein Knecht und dein Kind" (your servant and your child), and the Lord's reply echoes "my servant and my child." [28] Calan then promptly points out that the two words have little solid connection—beyond an alliterative one—and may well be mutually exclusive. He says of his servant Chus: ". . . yes, he could be my son if he were not my servant." [29] For Calan the idea of sonhood contradicts the idea of servitude, and he trains his "inquiring and investigating" mind on the question of what is the proper father-son (God-man) relationship.[30]

Noah's servile piety is unthinkable for Calan, and Barlach proceeds to illustrate the weakness of all Noah represents by laying bare his true relationship to his family and his god. As head of his family, Noah proves to be neither father nor lord. Actually he is the slave of his sons, of his wife, and of his own senses. His caution and fear of physical servitude under Calan preclude the possibility of spiritual freedom.[31] Noah is neither a good son nor a good servant of his god. When they stand face to face, Noah can scarcely recognize even his *former* father in him: "I'm confused, you were once my father, weren't you?" [32] And the Beggar-Lord replies: "You were once my son." Their connection seems all but dissolved. It is supported by a vague memory of the past, by the Lord's plaintive pleading for obedience, and by Noah's cautious anxiety lest he make a false step. It takes much wheedling and promises of reward, and even a childish refusal to eat, for the Lord to get his way and persuade Noah to build the ark. And once this is accomplished, he has to remind Noah that he is hungry.[33] Noah's god is no better father and lord than his one "servant and child."

These words have a different sound and content when they come from Calan's tongue. The conviction that he is a "Gotteskind" (child of god) and no servant governs his action through the whole play, the search for his god-father, and finally for the One.[34] As the search nears its end, a reversal takes place; Calan is transformed from lord into servant and beggar; and he suddenly becomes aware of his true relationship to Chus. At the close of Part IV he says, "Komm, Chus, mein Kind . . ." and ". . . komm Kind, komm Chus." [35] From this point on through Part V, scene 3, the already familiar words are dinned into our ears, reaching a crescendo in the following exchange:

CALAN: . . . Chus, mein Kind. (. . . Chus, my child.)
ZEBID: Dein Kind? Dein Knecht. (Your child? Your servant.)
CALAN: Ein Herr hat Knechte, ein Bettelmann nicht. (A lord has servants, a beggar doesn't.)[36]

Yet in the concluding scenes, after Calan says pointedly to Noah, "Ich . . . will sterben, wie es dem Sohn ansteht, der kein Knecht seines Vaters ist" (I intend to die as befits a son who is no servant of his father), it is as if the words had lost their meaning.[37] In union with a voiceless and formless god, Calan has entered a relationship inexpressible in plain familial terms. Such talk is left to Noah and his sons. It has served its purpose and exhausted itself.

Barlach's technique is one of stress and overstress. His manipulation of *Knecht* and *Kind* is analogous to his alliterative devices and also to Calan's "inquiring and investigating." Stress, repetition, and the cumulative force of sound build up anticipation and intensity in single passages and in the play as a whole to the very end, even after Calan claims he has given up his "Plappern über Gott" (prattling about god).[38] The alliteration is reminiscent of Old High German *Stabreim,* just as the vocabulary and syntax remind one of Luther, but neither is used out of love for tradition.

This would be like Noah's vain attempt to return to a safe but dead past. Rather, Calan and Barlach are pushing ahead to something new. The diction is plain and conservative in a revolutionary way. Barlach is well aware that his modern audience will notice the linguistic roughness and distortion resulting from the search for alliteration, and that the general effect will be unlikely to please.

As we have seen, *Die Sündflut* offers much evidence of Barlach's struggle with words. He works primarily with simple ones of no more than two syllables like *Hand, Fleisch, Schwert, Fraß, Friede,* etc., which he then repeats over and over with heavy emphasis. This everyday vocabulary becomes disturbing by its very simplicity. Through repetition and stress, the words are gradually isolated and stripped of their usual connotations. Eventually they become exhausted of meaning and dissolve, or as Barlach says of the word *Gott:* ". . . if one takes it repeatedly on the tongue, one makes a mess of stewed prunes out of it." [39] For instance, the *hand,* a central word and image in the drama is reduced, near the end, to fingers, which in turn are literally eaten away to the bone.

The general effect is quite different from that achieved by other linguistically radical writers of this century. Barlach is not concerned with nuances or stylized beauty. What results from his manipulation of words is something grotesque bordering on the absurd. Twice in his letters he maintains that *Die Sündflut* is full of humor and that theater directors have failed to note this.[40] The reason is that Barlach's humor is akin to the grotesque genius he admired in Alfred Kubin and others and which does not necessarily excite laughter. His aim is to discomfort or disconcert the listener.

III *Words as Witness to the Divine*

The rebellion of the word against itself is indeed a grotesque matter. Barlach's language works to expose itself as meaningless. Lazarowicz' comment about moving beyond words to images would be corroborated were it not for the fact that the exposure is repeated without ceasing. It is Barlach's "blessed curse" that he, like Wau in the novel *Der gestohlene Mond,* is condemned to go on making words despite the realization that they are worthless when measured against the divine. Wau says in conversation with his alter ego, Wahl: "Words . . . are the refuse of his [God's] greatness, the worthlessness of his worth, and where I cease to be, there the word finds its own end. What remains for me but to demonstrate His worth through my worthlessness? Therefore, keep making words, lots of them and fresh ones; there cannot be enough of those streaming and storming tones . . ."[41]

The strident theological argument between Calan and Noah suffers the same fate as the individual words. The ministers and their ladies misunderstood it because they failed to see that Barlach had chosen the insoluble problem of evil as his debate topic and did not intend to formulate an answer to it. Actually the argument becomes quite confused—and so do we—when, for instance, Noah finds himself defending the position of his impious opponent before the Lord. It is an argument with, and about, words like "good" and "evil," and although it underlies the central dialogue, it proves unimportant in itself when Calan announces the end of his prattling about god. But in fact he does not stop. When, in his physical blindness, he has his mystical vision, he begins again with a fresh vocabulary.

In Barlach's thinking, words are to the divine as surface is to space.[42] Ordinary human perception cannot take in the endless spaces of the universe, as Iver noted in *Der arme Vetter*. We see the stars as if they were all on a single surface and cannot distinguish differences in depth. The following passage from a letter written in 1932 makes the analogy clear:

. . . words do not remain the same for a second—one says the word "God," and everyone interprets it as he pleases. I am long since sick of the word, but it comes to my lips again and again. If I wanted to discuss the Ultimate, for which, in my opinion, man has no measure, just as he has no depth perspective when he looks into space with his physical eye—he sees only a single surface, on which the most distant stars seem to be situated beside the nearest—if I then wanted to debate word for word about the Ultimate, I would perhaps give preference to polytheism. Then, without blushing, one can speak of "the" god, who would of course be anthropomorphic. . . And yet again the power and witness of that which, by human standards, is the most sublime is inherent in the musical setting and text of "Heilig, heilig ist der Gott Zebaoth, und alle Lande sind seiner Ehre voll." Whoever hears it, has it, but whoever interprets it, only understands it and has a rubbish heap of musical and other technicalities in his hands.

Too many words already! [43]

To apply these ideas to the play: With words, as with a wood-carver's chisel, it is possible to chip away all that obscures the essence and to create thereby a three-dimensional whole. Barlach focuses attention on certain phrases, concepts, and images and builds up the pressure to what he would call the crystallization point where one must step back and view the product in its spatial dimensions as a "crystallized, firmly formed configuration." [44] In *Die Sündflut*, this point is reached at the end of Part IV and coincides with Calan's fall and awakening. Calan is transformed from wealthy master to beggar and father. His sensual, physical self ("Beschaffenheit") loses its former glory and becomes identified with the hunchbacked leper. He no longer dines in splendor but is now rather food for vermin. Calan's new awareness of himself and the world about him is followed immediately by his blinding and the revelation that his god has neither voice nor form. The sudden change is particularly forceful because Barlach's diction has succeeded in evoking the full physicality of things and senses with such intensity.

Barlach is not simply negating the world as a "badly ventilated narrow pass." His statement is that only through sharpened, critical awareness of the world, bad as it may be, can one attain the ultimate vision. It is important that only Calan and Awah—in her passive, naïve way—are completely open to sense experience. A scrutiny of the imagery dealing with eyes and sight, ears and hearing shows that Noah is continually afraid of his senses and what they tell him. It is characteristic of him that he fails to see things and that he often puts his hands over his ears. He is frightened by the sound of his own words and by the temptation his eyes offer him. His attitude is summed up in his treatment of the leper. He doesn't want to look at him and repeatedly shoos him away. It is precisely this caution which deafens and blinds him to the presence of the divine. Calan, on the other hand, is always testing, listening, looking, and asking to be shown.

The central idea of the play is contained in Calan's investigations and the discovery of his own creatural nature. This is his descent into hell. His experience is like Barlach's; he finds himself "directly on the brink of decay" but finds also that total despair can lead to highest certainty.[45] Noah and his sons avoid the issue and remain prisoners of the corrupt flesh. Calan proceeds to the final station where he is lashed to the leper. Then, with eyes and flesh gnawed away and freed from the tyranny of the senses, he achieves, through this experience of his own body, total acceptance and perception of his god as luminous presence.

Inquiring and investigating, therefore, do not in themselves lead to certainty or knowledge of the divine. Rather they lead to despair, confusion, and destruction if pursued incessantly. Yet, like the making of words, they are a necessary evil, working like an acid to eat away the dross and clear the way for the epiphany. The mystical vision turns out to be personal, inward experience, for which the potential has been there from the start. The paradox lies in the fact that Calan "sees" something that has no form and, after renouncing language, tries to describe in words something ineffable: God as pure, dynamic Becoming.

IV *Postscript on* Die gute Zeit *and* Der Graf von Ratzeburg

Die gute Zeit (*The Good Time,* 1929) is the last of Barlach's seven finished dramas, and the fourth of the group with mythic backgrounds. He worked on it at a time when the veterans' organization known as the "Stahlhelm" was barking at his heels and he was fighting to save his reputation and his war memorials.

The play itself lacks the balance and power of *Die Sündflut.* It attacks the moral degeneracy and hedonistic values of the 1920's and makes use of a parodistic language which sounds precious and highly mannered. In it we see two worlds and two ways of life. The first, the so-called good time, is represented by a colony of sensualists living in easy pleasure on a sunny shore. They practise the cult of "absolute insurance" ("absolute Versicherung" or "AV")—which simply means that the women see to it that they bear no children. Barlach, of course, abhors this static irresponsible existence.

The second, bad, time is the life of the impoverished hill people nearby. They know nothing of contraception and bring too many children into this "dog's life." By means of this contrast, Barlach demonstrates once more that good and bad are meaningless words. The hedonists and the suffering poor are equally guilty. The latter murder their offspring to keep the population down. Neither takes any responsibility, and the young primitives blame everything on their fathers.

Between these two worlds stands Celestine, a queen from a foreign land. She is pregnant with a child by a sick man. She must choose between abortion and bearing a degenerate heir. Barlach cuts the Gordian knot by letting her sacrifice her life—on a cross —out of consciousness of her own guilt and to save a young mountaineer who very much wants to live. Thus she creates the true good time within herself and dies to open the way for becoming and reality.[46]

This altruistic suicide by crucifixion serves as an unsatisfactory ending to a rather incoherent and probably experimental drama. The uncanny atmosphere and tone of the dialogue is unlike anything else Barlach wrote.

Heinrich, the title figure of *Der Graf von Ratzeburg (The Count of Ratzeburg)*, sacrifices himself in like manner. He suffers and dies vicariously for his bastard son after having passed through several stations on his road to perception and a new beginning. The road begins and ends in the city of Mölln. In the opening scene, Count Heinrich is at the pinnacle of his career and has just talked that city out of a piece of its land. The last words of the play describe how, many years later, he falls under the spears of a raging crowd of Möllners who are seeking vengeance for crimes committed by his villainous natural son.

Count Heinrich bears a strong resemblance to Calan in *Die Sündflut* in that he renounces worldly possessions and rethinks the relationship between lord and servant, as well as that between father and son. On the walk back from Mölln in scene 1, he suddenly begins to question the meaning of power, property, and authority. He soon sets off on a pilgrimage to the Holy Land and finds himself in actuality a beggar. Scene 4 opens in Smyrna, and he appears in chains, a galley slave of the Sultan.

Thus far the play reads like a historical drama based on events taking place around the year 1500. However, five scenes at the center of the work are located on Mount Sinai, where Count Heinrich stands by as a spectator, listening to dialogues between the ascetic Hilarion and various figures such as the ghosts of

Moses, Adam and Eve, and the fallen angel Marut. In fact, Adam and Eve and a character akin to Saint Christopher—called variously Offerus, Christoffer, and Christophorus—accompany him through the entire play. This strong element of fantasy and legend is not well integrated with the historical action and Count Heinrich's spiritual awakening. The best scenes are laid on German soil, in Ratzeburg and the neighboring city of Mölln. The remaining episodes seem designed as vehicles for deep and obscure speculations on the meaning of human suffering, fear, freedom, and other ethical issues.

The turgid style in which this is carried on may be seen in the following exchange. Hilarion speaks with the ghost of Moses about the Ten Commandments:

HILARION: God's stillness speaks louder than God's thunder, great Moses. It is not said: thou shalt; it is said: thou mayest.
MOSES *laughs:* May a man who cannot? Of course, many can who are supposed to.
HILARION: Those who are supposed to and can through their being able to, those the grave chews up, and all their being able is food for eating, permanence of inconstancy, emptying of nothingness, death of birth, and footstep in the desert sandstorm. Work of the soles, great Moses, not work of the soul.[47]

Der Graf von Ratzeburg appears as the last play in the edition of collected dramas, and in his introductory essay, the editor, Klaus Lazarowicz, treats it as if it were the summation of Barlach's artistry and wisdom. Actually the printed text is based on a preliminary draft found among Barlach's papers and dated 1927, two years before the publication of *Die gute Zeit*. Notations in the manuscript and other evidence show that he planned many additions and revisions. He carried these out later in a final draft, which, however, was lost in 1945.[48] In its present form, *Der Graf von Ratzeburg* is a loosely constructed drama overladen with symbolic characters and deeply felt but poorly articulated ideas. The attempt at high tragedy misses the mark. Barlach may have sensed this and withheld it from publication. To place it at the center of an interpretive essay, as Lazarowicz does, is to do him a disservice.

CHAPTER 5

Shadow and Sunlight:
Vision in Der blaue Boll

MOST interpretations of *Der blaue Boll* (1926) treat it as an obscure metaphysical thesis play. Articles such as " 'Der blaue Boll' and the New Man" [1] and books like Herbert Meier's *Der verborgene Gott: Studien zu den Dramen Ernst Barlachs* [2] may illuminate the philosophical aspect of the play, but they neglect other important questions. What, for instance, is the dramatic event? And has it any artistic merit?

When reduced to a bare ideological pronouncement, e.g., "It [a quote from the play allegedly containing its essence] confirms the transcendental imperative, revokes the tragic 'excarnation' and reiterates the law according to which the immanent self is the ground of the transcendent one," *Der blaue Boll* sounds trite and pompous.[3] When its characters are reduced to allegorical skeletons—Boll equals Everyman—the drama is unlikely to attract new readers. What needs to be known is that it is not just another late expressionist play about the New Man. It is, rather, an intricate, vivid, lively work of art and Barlach's best play.

To gain some insight into its workings, one must first recognize that Barlach is too much of an artist to be treated as a mediocre *Dichterdenker* (poet-thinker)—one of that peculiarly German tribe of lay theologians and amateur philosophers. The kernel of what *Der blaue Boll* has to say is not to be found in simplistic generalities about change and becoming, e.g., "Werden vollzieht sich unzeitig" [4] (Becoming takes place untimely), but in the theatrical events or "Bilder" (tableaus or scenes), in the intense visible representation of people, things, and actions.

It is also rich in verbal and visual comedy and is, in this respect, an improvement over *Die echten Sedemunds*, for the ludicrous element is comparatively subtle and perfectly integrated with the rest. Barlach's calm sense of humor informs the play, and part of

Boll's metamorphosis, evanescent as it may be, consists in his acquiring such a sense. *Der blaue Boll* shows evidence of the author's greater maturity and sureness of hand. Barlach had learned the trick of being "significant in a casual manner." [5]

By examining the two interrelated themes and complexes of imagery at the drama's core, one can discover its coherence and fine esthetic balance. The first theme may be called the alimentary vision. It finds expression in grotesque-comic references to flesh, teeth, mouth, food, and the digestive process. The second is the optical vision. It parallels the first on a higher plane, just as Boll's spiritual awakening parallels Grete Grüntal's physical disgust cure. It is more subtly presented but more important and has to do with visual perception, light, and eyes. The two strands are part of Boll's experience and are woven together to form a contrapuntal design throughout the play's seven scenes.

Upon close reading it becomes clear that Barlach is trying to dramatize the experience Geoffrey H. Hartman discerns in poems and poets of the nineteenth and twentieth centuries: "The mind, therefore, being most keenly aware through the dominant eye of that which is the cause of perception, pure representation will, at base, be the urge to construct the ideal system of symbols which relieves consciousness of the eyes' oppression but assures it of the eyes' luminosity." [6] We will see that Barlach provides such a set of symbols in the final scene of *Der blaue Boll*, where the issues of flesh and eye—and suicide—are resolved. The discussion of this crucial episode, however, requires a few preliminary comments.

The drama's basic figure is the confrontation and mingling of opposites. This takes place repeatedly in the action; it can be seen in individual characters as well as in the mingling of realistic, supernatural, comic, and serious elements. Apostolic Community and Friendly Devil's Kitchen (a bar) face each other across a narrow street. Manor house and piggery, church and seduction are brought together in the first scene. The apoplectic, and therefore blue, Squire Boll and young Grete Grüntal, the swineherd's wife, meet here and join in a common aim: to do away with flesh and, it seems, to indulge it too. He intends to jump from the church tower; she wishes to poison her children and hints at favors she will grant if Boll procures the poison. The remainder of the play shows, first, how Boll helps restore her to sanity and acceptance of her carnal state and, second, how she returns the favor. Grete's transformation is visceral; Boll's cure has to do with the body but is sublimated and presented finally in visual and spiritual terms. Grete survives her crisis with the help of the strangely angelic devil Elias, the innkeeper. Boll is helped by "ein Herr" (gentleman or lord), who, though hobbled by a cloven hoof, is taken by some to be the Lord.[7] As in all of Barlach's good plays, it is a matter of relative proportion and emphasis rather than clear distinction.

The verbal action follows a similar pattern. As in *Die Sündflut*, Barlach stresses certain words: "becoming," "responsibility," "falling," "eating," "must," "will," and "Jeder ist sich selbst der Nächste" (Charity begins at home). Characters of the most varied sort bandy about these phrases. Boll introduces some; one we hear first from the sectarian watchmaker Virgin. Then the Herr, the Apostolic Congregation, the devil Elias, shoemaker Holtfreter, and the drunken, bigoted Cousin Otto adopt and repeat them. The audience must ask itself what they mean and how they are interconnected. Boll himself does not find the answers until the end, and then they are couched in allusive seemingly casual images and words.

In the shifts of proportion and emphasis lies Barlach's mastery. Through the entire play, Boll hangs between two existences. He finds himself in the same situation as Barlach's sculptured figures: "in the middle ground between a whence? and a whither?"[8] When the action begins, Boll has already suffered the shock of self-recognition and can no longer take himself for granted. He has seen that there is something radically wrong with Boll the estate owner. To Frau Boll's and Cousin Otto's dismay, he begins to inquire and investigate, and he speaks of himself in the third person. He soon reaches the conclusion that suicide provides the only means for change.

Speaking in the irate tone one would use to complain about traffic conditions or clogged sewers, Boll says in scene 1 to the mayor of Sternberg:

Part? I'm out after the whole today. Parts—let's forget parts. Is this right, I ask you, Mr. Mayor? Better to live than die, that's the issue. What awful misfits we creatures are in this existence—how are we brought into this bestial life—are we asked, do we agree to it? Bestial life—how so? Aren't we well off, better, better yet, and even better than that—and suddenly, what do I see—it stops getting better and gets bad, worse, and worse than that. What a shabby impropriety—look, Pastor, at that trap, its joints are oiled, its jaws are sharp and they're snapping at our flesh and bone! Wham! and then we've got to hold still. First we live high, too high, and then . . . well, that's how it is.[9]

Boll is at odds with himself and about to kill himself in order to escape the trap. The very fact that he is re-examining his life indicates that he has a new and clearer viewpoint. But what he sees drives him further into despair. His visual and spiritual disgust cure has started.

Of character development in the usual sense there is little evidence. For the play does not concern a new or old Boll but rather the complicated circumstances surrounding his inner awakening and the subtle shift of perspective which reveals to him the way out of his dilemma. Of all of Barlach's dramas, *Der blaue Boll* is at once the subtlest and most vivid. It is so well rounded that it offers no easy handholds for interpretation. The discursive, yet comic and unreliable, comments of devil and Herr tend to cancel each other out. Also the central theme is embellished by a number of vaguely similar events: Grete, Frau Boll, and Cousin Otto all change in some way, however banal it may be. These variations and commentaries tend to muddy rather than clarify the issues. There is much prattling about becoming. Not until the last scene does silence replace the chatter—momentarily, to be sure—and the concept become reality.

I *Scene 7 of* Der blaue Boll

The scenes, or "Bilder," of the play contain sharply outlined visual effects, on which the characters' comments invite us to speculate. Their words, in accordance with Barlach's conviction that the word is at best a crutch for those satisfied to limp, only complement the play of light, spatial relationships, and eyes. They lend the action an air of mystery and metaphysical import. In fact, one might read *Der blaue Boll* as a mystery play by forcing the events into a pattern of death, descent into hell, resurrection, and crass comic interludes. For Barlach is generous with material suggestive of the supernatural. Yet he is also careful to keep things in a state of suspension by counterbalancing these flashes of transcendence with reminders that his characters and their actions are all too human. For example, the fantasies in scene 6 may be an apocalyptic vision of suffering sinners in hell or a delirious dream in the mind of a drunken woman. Like the Herr at the end, Barlach warns us against too much speculation with a "Mehr ist vom Übel" (More cometh from evil).[10]

Consequently, instead of extrapolating the play's meaning from discursive remarks on becoming, we will consider the dramatic event in scene 7. It is a repetition in altered form of the events in the preceding scenes; and it has to do with eyes, vision, and flesh —Barlach's lifelong preoccupations.

The setting is inside the Gothic church which has figured in all but two scenes. The scenery is sparse to the point of abstraction; we see one pillar, one window, one bench, and an apostle carved in wood. The morning sun shines on the apostle. As the curtain rises, Boll is walking up and down. Grete Grüntal, the swineherd's wife, lies sleeping. Boll is about to send her back—restored and sane—to husband and children. Grete wakes up, and in the course of the conversation about the events of the night before she is distracted by the statue. The following apparently incidental exchange ensues (note the frequency of the words "look" and "see"):

GRETE *looks back and forth between the figure of the apostle and Boll, laughs:* How he looks, how you both look! The sun is shining in his face and he has goggle eyes, wide open—is he hunting lice, or why is he fumbling in his beard?
BOLL: Him? Why yes, him! Look, now it's shining on my face, and a shadowy Boll is growing on the wall, the wooden saint and my shadow stand face to face, and you can easily see what kind of flesh they are cast from. Of course, once upon a time he was in the flesh, and I am still—look at that, Grete.
GRETE: He closes his mouth and his eyes gleam.
BOLL: Glow, glow—and mine?
GRETE: Yours—oh, blue Boll, they're not your best ornament. They are closed over by blinds, blinds, so that you should be ashamed to look out of them. Otherwise, your eyes are proper eyes, but they have sneaked off behind thick walnut shells. He has a mouth, but he keeps it shut.

BOLL: . . . and mine?

GRETE: Your mouth? Boll, yours isn't bad, good for yawning and showing teeth and for providing all sorts of offal for your teeth. But your teeth are very good. They can handle their share—he, look over there, what hollow cheeks, no room any more for teeth. . . . Perhaps his eyes glow because he has no teeth and can be on the lookout for other things beside meat.[11]

The silent but eloquent apostle dominates the whole scene. Eyes, teeth, and shadows speak louder than words.

Driven to despair by the juxtaposition of his shadow and the "Petermännchen"[12] or apostle, Boll then announces by indirection his intention to commit suicide.[13] Then suddenly—perhaps he moves his head a bit—Grete drops the thread of conversation and notes: "When the sun shines in your eyes, they glow better than his, I see that clearly when I look close."[14] And Boll replies: "No wonder—can he do anything with his eyes but let them be seen—but I do my own seeing and see you sitting there and hear you speaking the truth, and you see out of your eyes like an intact and healthy woman." The dialogue ends when Boll repeats the leitmotif: "Jeder ist sich selbst der Nächste" (Charity begins at home).

Spoken here for the last time, the phrase acquires new meaning. It no longer suggests schizophrenia, as it did in scene 1. It does not cynically recognize the selfishness of all human beings, as it did when spoken by Elias. Nor does it bemoan the isolation of the individual. Boll has passed through these stages. Rather, it signifies a new egocentricity, and with it Boll affirms the integrity of his self.

The rest of the scene tells of Cousin Otto's stroke and death and of Frau Boll's act of humility. She kisses Grete's hand. Boll looks on both these events as modes of becoming, but they are not sufficient for him. Even though he continues to speak of suicide and seems about to follow the Herr's suggestion that he do it now, his point of view has already changed and another decision has ripened within him. He confronts the apostle with new self-assurance and says: "Look, friends, see the old sourpuss—a little while ago I was almost afraid of his wooden grandezza, but now I am standing with unusual indifference ["mit seltener Pomadigkeit"] before him. I can show you my teeth . . ."[15] It remains only for the Herr to force Boll to an overt decision against suicide as too primitive a mode of becoming.

One wonders why Barlach resorts to this complicated interplay of eyes, teeth, light, and shadow if he aims only to show the resolution of the conflict between body and spirit[16] or between free will and necessity. Reference to similar passages and parallels will suggest what meaning should be attached to these images and what lies behind them. For instance, the wooden apostle, called a "Petermännchen," has its counterpart in the Gothic Christ figure which dominates scene 6 of *Die echten Sedemunds*. This, in turn, is related to the gigantic crucifix Barlach saw in the church at Güstrow. He writes in 1912 of "the church on the marketplace where . . . the gigantic crucifix stands, from medieval times when men conceived of themselves and their existence more mythically. . . . He stands again now like a hieroglyph and preaches that there is something other than flesh and bone." [17] For Barlach the dramatist, on the other hand, the statue is a hieroglyph in a system of symbols, and the reader is struck when, in *Der arme Vetter*, Siebenmark utters the word "Petermännchen"— later "Stehaufmännchen" ("tumbler doll" or possibly "resurrected manikin")—in a situation like Boll's. Siebenmark admits his inability to emulate Hans Iver, the saintly suicide, and says with sarcastic indifference: "I lack that reflected splendor from the beyond, that's the trouble! I am incapable of negotiating bows in any direction before Peter-manikins in spiritual halos." [18]

As usual in Barlach's finished works, the unambiguous statement of a letter or prose sketch is repeated with an ironic irreverent twist, perhaps to preserve the esthetic equilibrium. Christ and his apostle are associated with tumbler dolls (roly-polys), just as a deep-sounding bit of metaphysical speculation reappears in a novel as a product of confused thinking.[19]

Siebenmark and Boll have a good deal more in common. They discover the full meaning of "Jeder ist sich selbst der Nächste." Both may bow initially before the toothless, ascetic spirituality of their respective "Petermännchen," and each may come close to suicide in his extremity; yet each undergoes a change—largely a change in perspective—and learns to see and accept. Also, neither denies his selfhood; and neither gives up carnal and material things.

The dramatic event is more clearly outlined in *Der blaue Boll* than in the earlier play. For Boll dominates the action, and the metamorphoses of Otto and Grete have only suggestive force. Grete's experience sets the pattern. Overnight she recovers from her insane disgust with flesh and accepts her life in the piggery. Similarly, in scene 7, Boll first sees himself solely as a shadow in this vale of misery and then is set free to begin again. The dramatic events of earlier scenes prepare for this; each is a rehearsal for the crisis.

The first event brings together the issues of perception (mist and blurred perspective),[20] selfhood, and flesh ("Away with flesh").[21] Boll passes through a period of vacillation and disgust with himself but emerges from the fog of confusion with the decision to follow Grete into the church tower.[22] In scene 2 he again despairs and loses direction but regains perspective with a scornful glance from the tower upon the town and with the assumption of responsibility for Grete.[23]

In scene 3, he has, once more, admittedly "lost his way."[24] Both inwardly and in his movements on the stage he is running back and forth, apparently getting nowhere. He fails in his mission to get the poison, and because of his meandering he misses his dinner engagement altogether. He even loses Grete to the devil Elias. In short, he has no direction. Near the end of scene 4 he says: "Away with Boll—and he cannot even ask whether he wants or has to? Don't I have the bit between my teeth? What's the use—he has to wait until it pulls and shows where the trip is heading."[25]

Finally, in scene 5, the bit begins to twitch and hurt. His responsibility for Grete, so casually assumed, turns out to be a matter of life and death. And the "bitter family resemblance" between himself and Cousin Otto shames and disgusts him so that he announces his decision—by repeating the word "fall" as often as he does "see" later on—to throw himself from the church tower.

Scene 6 shows us Grete's recovery by means of a phantasmagory. And the final scene describes how Boll finds his direction and ceases to feel the bit. As it opens, he is again, literally, walking back and forth, whereas the interior of the Gothic church seems to be shooting upward like "stone rockets." [26] Thus Squire Boll stands on the brink of death ("ganz hart und unmittelbar am Verwesen")[27] at the intersection of two sets of forces: an earthly one that has been driving him back and forth in an aimless way and another, religious one which invites him to rise rapidly upward and fall equally fast from the tower. There seems to be no compromise or middle ground between the two, except in Boll himself.

The sight of his shadow on the wall revolts him as strongly as did the "bitter family resemblance." With merciless precision the sunlight paints this simple picture of Boll's inescapable carnal condition. But then the rays of the sun unexpectedly reveal to Grete the glow, or luminosity, of his eyes. In other words, from one point of view the sunlight reduces Boll to an ugly black mark or "a black, heavy piece of night," [28] as he pictures his body falling from the tower. Without the resonant response from Grete, he cannot see what the sun's direct rays do to him and his eyes. They illuminate and bring forth his share, however small, in divinity, as well as the dignity of the human body and particularly of the eye, which is more than an organ of vision. Boll's ultimate acceptance is thus the result of an indirect, symbolic perception that takes place when his eyes meet Grete's. In *Der blaue Boll* and elsewhere Barlach often tries to show that human values are revealed only when one sees rays from the beyond reflected and refracted in others.[29]

II *The Image of the Shadow in* Seespeck *and Elsewhere*

To justify such emphasis on a single event in *Der blaue Boll* and to give further content to the concepts "New Man" and "conversion," we need to look at certain other works. The most appropriate would be *Die Sündflut,* the immediate predecessor of *Der blaue Boll.* On the surface the two are quite dissimilar. The final scene of *Die Sündflut* is dark, bloody, and gruesome. Calan also plans suicide; he is made painfully aware of his carnal state when Noah's sons lash him to the leper and leave him to be devoured by vermin and drowned; and he experiences a luminous epiphany.

Epiphanous visions are not granted to all Barlach's heroes. In *Der tote Tag,* the son never emerges from his state of suspension

between two existences—childhood and manhood, in oversimpli-
fied terms. He longs to see what the sun can see without going
blind, but he is trapped by the fog of his own incapacity to act or
create.[30] His last day, too, hangs dead between heaven and earth,
and the sun never breaks through.[31] He recognizes only his own
lack of perception and kills himself. He says of his walk through
the mist: "I was walking with open eyes and could see how blind
I was, for this was a blindness that doesn't come from the eyes,
but rather the other kind that makes the best eyes unseeing."[32]

Der Findling contains a comment which is poorly integrated
into the play but which, better than any other passage, makes
clear the meaning of shadows. "They say that the sun paints speaking images with sharp shadows, and yet I saw the shadow of a
horse on whose tail the sun was shining, and it had the shape of
a pig. Perhaps all of us here have the sun shining on our tails, and
our shadows play a mockery before us."[33]

The fragmentary novel *Der gestohlene Mond* stops short of the
ultimate vision. In a passage which lurks behind the actions and
thoughts of Wau, the central figure, through the remainder of the
book, we read of the "merciless perception" he derives from the
following momentary apparition:

A shadow had stood there which proceeded from him, pierced the
clouds, hid the moon, and stretched out infinitely far into the universe,
filled it in fact. . . . And it was his shadow, as he recognized by its
step. . . . During the timeless moment of his vision he had perceived
one more thing: the shadow of a body in the infinity of space, a form
like the sun peculiarly distorted, glowing, but dimmed as if by haze,
which made strange movements and trembled as if in a spasm—far, far
out, way over and beyond the sun.[34]

The perception is merciless because the luminous shape (the cosmic enlargement of his heart) remains cloaked in haze. Wau has
no vis-à-vis like Grete. He tries to articulate the experience and to
infuse it with religious meaning but grows silent just as the crucial
word is coming to his lips. Wau and Wahl, his alter ego, speak as
one spirit: " 'For whether it is your shadow or you are its shadow,
the only thing that matters is that there is Being and a permeation
of the universe with . . .'—'With?,' came the question. 'With . . .
think it over before you say anything about it. Stop and keep

still.'" [35] Both are ashamed of their speculative excesses and agree never again to speak of such things.

Barlach's earlier, autobiographical novel *Seespeck* also treats again and again of shadows. It is a better aid to the understanding of *Der blaue Boll*, scene 7, because, though the author never released all of it for publication, it is at least a full torso, and, as in *Der blaue Boll*, the cosmic overtones are muted. Like the play, *Seespeck* is constructed as a series of rounded episodes, or stations, leading ultimately to a new mode of vision, acceptance, and a new beginning.

Seespeck knows that he has lost his way. Brief moments of insight, a series of epiphanies, make him aware of his plight. He asks himself: Where do I belong? And then he begins to inquire and investigate. As the action progresses, we see that he is really asking: How can I escape myself? He looks back to his childhood, thinks of marriage, and tries to find release in friendship, religion, music, and complete devotion to visual experiences. But in each case some optical effect blocks the way and drives him back to his original state, suspended in a rootless existence. His role in life seems to be that of an "improper guest" ("ungehöriger Gast").[36] Like Boll, he is trapped and isolated. "Now . . . it seemed to him as if he were walking along a long plank and could find no exit anywhere, and he had a suspicion that the plank was running in a circle, and he with it." [37]

In this peculiar limbo, Seespeck is easily transported outside himself by fleeting sense impressions, such as the three notes of a music box or a glimpse of a girl walking down the street. But this is further evidence of his confusion and leads him only deeper into despondency.[38] Right after the reverie inspired by the music box, he meets a prostitute and suffers an odd defeat. When she fails to show a trace of hardness or indecency, he flees in disarray and disgust at himself. She lets him out of her sight like "a cool, gray, formless shadow." [39] His nausea and anxiety reach panic proportions when he thinks he sees the grotesque baker Buur, a sharp reminder of his own condition.

This confrontation with the prostitute is one of a series of episodes in which Seespeck is betrayed and trapped by his eyes. "And in his bosom our good Seespeck became afraid on account of all these visual experiences. What did it mean when he had to admit to himself that his eyes or his senses seemed to have reached the ultimate limit where, if he penetrated further, clear, naked being had to reveal itself without illusion or veil." [40]

Repeatedly, the object of his observation changes its aspect like a drawing in which the perspectives shift as one stares at it; and he finds that his hungry eyes have made him a slave to naked hideousness. For instance, at the end of Chapter 2 he dreams of looking through the rear window of a moving coach and sees a church tower approaching; or, with a slight change in point of view, Seespeck and his two friends on a walk become "dolls trampling in response to a mysterious direction and compulsion in an indeterminate area between the real starry sky and its reflection, on a paper-thin, unsupported middle ground." [41]

Each of the first four chapters ends with such an event, as if to prove to Seespeck that he is looking at things the wrong way. At the end of Chapter 3, a simple optical phenomenon, the image of a candle flame inverted and projected onto a wall by a lens, turns his stomach and forces him to abandon his friends. These attacks of vertigo and nausea are not simply physical. They are accompanied by guilt feelings of an unspecified nature and by Seespeck's conviction that he has become a shadow, which he regards as emblematic of his own disgrace. [42] The hero of Adalbert von Chamisso's *Peter Schlemihl* likewise suffers shame and ostracism, but in his case it is for lack of a shadow. Elias accuses Boll of being only half a man, and this is the message that Seespeck's shadow transmits to him. [43]

The turning point, when the heap of experiences suddenly crystallizes into true perception, comes in the second of two Däubler chapters (6). Seespeck believes he has found "one piece or more of my *Doppelgänger*" in the person of Däubler. [44] The latter, like Grete and the apostle in *Der blaue Boll*, catalyzes the ultimate vision. And again a subtle change in lighting is the final cause. Seespeck, in his customary shadowy capacity, sits as a spectator and outsider while Däubler and the doctor conduct a deep philosophical discussion on the "salvation and future of the world." [45] The argument between the two—the latter a liberal bourgeois hedonist, the former a high priest and prophet of otherworldliness —treats of familiar issues: personality, ego, shadow, and light. [46] But Seespeck does not listen. Their remarks, like those on becoming in *Der blaue Boll,* are simply an accompaniment to his visual experiences. As usual, they overwhelm him, but then we read the following:

. . . and yet in the end it was Seespeck's old friend, the dim light of the autumn afternoon, that changed the coloration of the doctor's or of Däubler's super-humanity to friendly brotherliness. He was not inferior to them, he felt. . . . It inspired him to wish to accomplish something for his own part, which would be the equivalent of these emanations from them. . . . Very slight, very modest, but forever valid, something whole. . . . "Nothing but myself, but that without crack or blemish, the ego that holds everything secure in itself," such was his momentary inner illumination.[47]

This fleeting inner gleam leads Seespeck in the next, and last, chapter to the potter's workshop in Güstrow and a new career as an artist. As in *Der blaue Boll,* the change is slight. He knows that he will never escape from himself, that "Jeder ist sich selbst der Nächste," but he refuses to take refuge in the old shadow existence. Instead, "with unusual indifference," he represents himself to his prospective neighbors as the most isolated of humans—a professional executioner. This is the vivid, comic extension of the decision inspired by the new look at Däubler and the doctor. The change of light, then, accomplishes two things. It reduces Däubler to human proportions and raises Seespeck's self-esteem. This is essentially the same event that takes place in scene 7 of *Der blaue Boll,* where Boll looks at the apostle not with disrespect but at least on even terms.

The sight of Däubler leads to this climactic recognition, because in the years around 1914 Barlach was engaged in a search for the distinction between his own and his friend's mode of vision. Chapter 1 of this study mentions Barlach's ambivalent feelings toward Theodor Däubler and cites a letter in which we find the ideas behind Seespeck's insight. "I consider him . . . a stranger on this earth, he is prodigious, . . . he is a . . . celestial conflagration, but warm mild sunshine contains (for my sensibility) the stronger grace. . . . He has organs that may grasp colors and forms, but no eyes, not my kind anyway." [48] And in "Diario Däubler" he writes, "He would like to murder sight, because he knows that light, the better light, will create its own eyes which will suit it better." [49]

In the novel, the precise nature of Seespeck's reorientation is not clearly articulated. For conceptual language, as far as Barlach is concerned, cannot tell us what happens here. Both Boll and Seespeck finally discover and accept their position in the logically contradictory but creative center between two poles represented by the doctor and Däubler, or the devil Elias and the Herr. We are concerned here with the paradox of simultaneous surrender and intensification of the ego. The new Boll can scoff at the apostle and then kneel before him without inner contradiction. Again and again in his correspondence and in his writings, Barlach tries to communicate this experience. He writes with reference to Calan in *The Flood*: "I grasp, no, I am grasped in my best moments by the idea of depersonalization, of absorption into something higher, I call it: the happiness of self-conquest, in which full consciousness of the ego is contained and preserved." [50]

Seespeck and all the kindred figures in Barlach's works feel at the outset that they live on the brink of physical corruption and yearn to escape this vale of tears. Yet each learns that he belongs here and that to escape into blindness, death, or transcendence is wrong. They inquire and investigate with eyes open and senses alert. In the end, the eye becomes a source of light, not just an organ of vision; merciless perception of reality becomes creative vision; and the ego is transformed from shadow to radiant plastic wholeness.

A momentary illumination heals the rift. Barlach repeatedly pondered this phenomenon from his personal experience. In 1915 he wrote in a letter:

I see forms and colors, know it is inspired but configured light, and can be confident that my senses are not deceiving me with delight or repugnance; and lo and behold, there is a transformation of the spirit. I am like a lover who would like to worship the Creator, but since my eyes and nerves, my whole conscious sensory capacity, are inclined to worship and gratitude, I stick with my gratitude to the creature, which provides me with a sign, as is fitting for a sacrament. No need for meditation, one has to believe, and thus one is free of one's self (I am speaking about me), consciousness can and must vanish, I am set free like an unhaltered horse on the meadow of infinity. . . . That the harness is put on again cannot prevent me from knowing that it was a lightning flash of the beyond, the "I" had been impersonal, delimited, and yet it had remained and was not dispersed.[51]

This is what happens to Boll. Barlach says expressly of him that he does not succeed in moving over and beyond himself. He accepts the harness again and returns to his estate, fortified by "knowledge of salvation and sanctity." [52]

Through reference to Barlach's writing over many years and by suggesting a certain distribution of emphasis, I have tried in the foregoing remarks to illuminate the suggestive but not self-explanatory final scene in *Der blaue Boll* and to offer clues for deciphering Barlachian hieroglyphs wherever they may appear. The following characteristic quote should now seem less arcane: "The nature of being is obscure because we have eyes with which we try to understand it, hence it is good that there is vision which makes all understanding superfluous." [53]

III *Postscript on* Der gestohlene Mond

In the years 1936 and 1937, Barlach worked on a novel entitled *Der gestohlene Mond*. It never reached completion. Like Kafka's *Castle* and Musil's *Man without Qualities*, with which Barlach's book can be compared, it is an experimental work and by its very nature resists a satisfactory conclusion. All three are so-called anti-novels, which throw not only the image of man but also the very possibility of narration into question.

The thread of the action—Wau's implication in the destinies of an unwed mother and his alter ego Wahl—serves only as the barest excuse for dialogues and monologues, which circle about such themes as guilt, responsibility, good and evil, suffering, and joy, and for pyrotechnic displays of verbal virtuosity in descriptions of all kinds. Barlach carries his stylistic principle of being significant in a casual way to new extremes.

To be sure, Wau, outwardly a quite unexceptional upper-middle-class citizen, is subject to mystical, visionary experiences like Boll's or Seespeck's. He calls them "presences" ("Gegenwärtigkeiten"),[54] but the remainder of the book consists largely of essayistic meditations, sometimes in dialogue form, and exercises in precise and exhaustive description of peripheral details. Wau is constantly engaged in what he calls "Übung des Betrachtens" (practice in contemplation)[55] and achieves results no more concrete than emerge from the dialogue between Calan and Noah or Däubler and the doctor. Wau never gives up, however, even though each time he comes full circle and finds "everything much worse than before." [56]

This ragging, terrier-like style of thought leads Wau to the outer limits where he finds himself, like Seespeck, an alien shadowy spectator looking at the world and himself. And neither offers a pleasing prospect. "Why, you would be nothing more than the excrement of your real being," is one crass formulation.[57] The following nearly untranslatable passage from the beginning of the ninth chapter will give an inkling of how the novel works and of the burdens it imposes on the reader:

If incongruities of undetermined nature were all too surely inherent in the legitimate stability of things, . . . then with such practice in reflection this legitimate stability of things itself began to crack, and its firmness became doubtful. What sort of stability was this that was so shot through with palpable incongruities! Now and then dreams produced shocks lasting for days, and so Wau awoke one morning benumbed and slightly feverish with the recollection of a dreamed yet very forcible experience. It caused him to stand before a chamber or small room and to perceive or discover that, piled up or stowed, packed and stacked like rubbish in the corners, nothing but broken phonograph records filled it; he knew also, but from an infusion of knowledge, as often happens in dreams, that all these records were once the phases of his life to date and, now destroyed and as trifles and inconsequential remnants, did not signify but simply intimated nothing other than broken antecedencies. There was no one present who spoke, saying that the past was, or was supposed to be, meaningless, but the broken state of the records convinced him of it with a stronger than oral eloquence . . .[58]

In the same highly indirect way, the rest of the chapter dwells on how Wau hides his moody despair from his housekeeper (". . . he was successful in taking the greatest pains with the most punctilious unobtrusiveness . . .")[59] and speculates in a fruitless way on the questions of guilt, infinity, and theodicy. Not only this section, but the whole book is an attempt to give artistic form to a vision of life which sees it as a room full of broken records and yet assumes that it nevertheless has order and meaning. The manuscript breaks off while the "palpable incongruities" dominate the scene.

CHAPTER 6

The Use and Abuse of the Past

IN THE case of Barlach's literary work, the hunt for sources and ties with the past tends to defeat itself. In looking for specific literary sources, it threatens to lose itself in a maze of rejected possibilities and farfetched conjecture. This inquiry points to likely models but then has to back off and admit that, at best, Barlach has obscured, distorted, even perverted them. In the end it retreats to the surmise that living individuals, certain buildings, and landscapes have far more to do with the genesis of a Barlach play than do books. Yet, however tenuous the ties with the past and however negative the results of this investigation, there does emerge a clear and illuminating outline of Barlach's attitudes toward tradition. We can also discern a pattern in his ways of using it to his own artistic ends.

Any attempt to place him in the broader literary or dramatic tradition is also in danger of running aground on any of several shoals. Barlach isolated himself, physically at least, from the intellectual and artistic world of his time. The art industry of Berlin—the theater and artistic cliques—were so uncongenial that he moved to the small Mecklenburg city of Güstrow in 1910 and later declined the offer of a professorship in order to stay there. All his important plays were completed after this retreat. Barlach was no theatergoer, nor was he an avid reader of plays. His drama seems to draw more heavily on nineteenth-century narrative prose and *Faust* than on the expressionist pantheon: *Büchner*, Strindberg, Wedekind.

Nor is his work experimental in the accepted post-Brechtian sense. Nevertheless it is unique; with no detectable break in style, a single play may read like a contemporary absurd piece and at the same time combine nineteenth-century elements with structural details and themes reminiscent of medieval mystery plays and the mystical writings of Böhme or Meister Eckhart. There is no published evidence outside the plays themselves to indicate that Barlach had any close acquaintance with these things, or even that he went to church.

In fact, the one word which best characterizes his attitude toward tradition and contemporary idols is impiety. Barlach liked to debunk. And much of his work aims to do this. It is a primary source of humor as, for instance, when he presents Noah as a henpecked weakling or in *Die echten Sedemunds* exposes the shortsightedness of the anti-bourgeois crusading cultist. Even Goethe is not spared the treatment. Failure to appreciate this caustic side of Barlach has led his critics to read him like a religious philosopher and theater directors to cut the comic-grotesque heart out of his plays.

This basic impiety is reflected in the absence of allegiance to any one tradition or period and in the way Barlach delights in the dissonance produced by mixing disparate elements. His relationship to tradition is thus more complicated and original than that of any other recognized writer for the theater in the years from 1910 to 1930. Barlach was not modern, as the term was understood in the 1920's. Directors sensed that his plays were revolutionary but missed the point that Barlach was a conservative revolutionary. He stands closer to the writers of medieval mysteries, say, than to Georg Kaiser, closer to Gothic art than to Picasso.

Symptomatic of his complicated relationship to tradition is the following list, culled from reviews and articles, of works and authors who may have influenced Barlach, or with whom he might be compared: *Fastnachtspiele* (Shrovetide plays), Byron, Samuel Beckett, Hamsun, Paul Kornfeld, Goethe's *Faust*, Brecht, Camus, Zacharias Werner, Wedekind, Werfel, and Raabe.

I Books and Real Life

An equally varied and inconclusive picture is offered by Barlach's own reading. The trouble is that many books and authors of consequence for his work are mentioned only in passing, or not at all, in his published letters and diaries. In his early years he read what might be expected of a middle-class German youth of the late 1880's and the 1890's: patriotic historical novels (Willibald Alexis), Gustav Freytag's *Bilder aus der deutschen Vergangen-*

heit, adventure novels like the *Leatherstocking Tales,* travel books (e.g., Seume, *Spaziergang nach Syrakus*), Carlyle, Charles Kingsley (*Briefe und Gedenkblätter*), Zola, and Maupassant.

Apart from some entertaining and edifying reading in the years up to 1906, there are three important items: Goethe's *Faust,* the novels of Jean Paul, and *Hanneles Himmelfahrt* by Hauptmann. Goethe occupied him all his life.[1] To acquire a taste and understanding for Jean Paul, however, was the work of several years. And watching Hauptmann's play at Dresden in 1894 was an intoxicating experience: "I feel like a spirit that has stripped off its earthly raiment and is flying about on free wings, hovering in 'dim moonlight' and over 'mountain heights.' " [2] These verbal allusions to Faust's opening monologue reflect Barlach's preoccupation with Goethe and perhaps his indentification with Faust. In 1893 he writes: "I don't read much, but Goethe grips me again and again with his *Faust,* I often spend a whole evening brooding over a single line and still can't get past it." [3]

In the years from 1906 to the end of the World War I, Barlach documented his continued preoccupation with Goethe and mentioned his translation of *Le Neveu de Rameau* in connection with Thomas Mann's *Tonio Kröger.*[4] What leads him to comment on these two works is the picture, common to both, of the artist as a bastard nature—half bourgeois, half bohemian. Also in the war years he began to read works of the Chinese poet-philosophers such as Klabund's adaptation of Li-Tai-Pe and translations of Dschuang Si and Lia-Sse. These books, too, provided a standpoint for Barlach's new look at European middle-class culture. He finds them full of Barlach and even thinks of Jean Paul as Chinese. Both the Chinese and Jean Paul have the style of deceptive realism which he admired. "I am making good progress with Jean Paul. He always seems Chinese to me. . . . It is the same reality and again the same unreality of things," he commented in conversation.[5]

In the long diary Barlach kept during the war years ("Güstrower Tagebuch," 1914–17) he mentions several works and authors. Some, like *The Pickwick Papers,* were seemingly chosen because they would entertain his mother and son when read aloud. The remainder looks like a random selection from whatever happened to fall into his hand: the *Eddas,* Eichendorff's *Taugenichts,*

Dostoyevsky, and Claudel's *Annonce faite à Marie*. The single
piece of literature he comments seriously upon is Gottfried Keller's *Der grüne Heinrich*. He came across it around 1916 and described it as "a slice through life. One sees the bowels while
they're still quivering." [6] Barlach was doubtlessly first captivated
by a feeling of personal affinity with Heinrich Lee, who, like himself, had to grow up without a father and suffered much as an art
student. In later years, Barlach went so far as to mention Keller's
work together with Goethe's *Die Leiden des jungen Werthers* as
examples of perfect prose. [7]

Keller and Barlach have much in common: bourgeois realism,
respect for the niceties of the German language, inclination toward provincial backgrounds, and a fondness for grotesque humor. And this is what Barlach found in Keller, namely a reflection
of himself in mid-career. Yet Keller leaves no discernible imprint
on Barlach's writings, which would presumably have turned out
the same, no matter what he read.

The only play clearly based on an earlier source is *Die Sündflut*
(1924), and it takes from the Bible very little besides some of its
characters, the incident of the Flood, and variations on the Book
of Job. Barlach's language is so singular that verbal echos from
other authors stand out vividly. But aside from an elusive hint of
Nietzschean diction (*Zarathustra*) detectable in *Die Sündflut*,
there remain but a few phrases, such as the mystical light imagery
at the end, which can be traced to earlier sources. In what seems a
calculated attempt to keep the audience guessing, Barlach puts
the Mephistophelian words "förderlich und dienstlich" ("useful
and dutiful") into the mouth of the ambiguous figure of the
"Herr" in *Der blaue Boll* (1926). [8] Yet the latter play is more Faustian in spirit than Hofmannsthal's *Der Tor und der Tod* or Werfel's *Spiegelmensch*, verse dramas whose language often betrays a
far larger debt to Goethe.

Barlach was not so isolated that he lacked connections with
other writers. Specifically, Moeller van den Bruck (1876–1925)
and Theodor Däubler (1876–1934) remained in close touch with
him until their deaths. Yet of Moeller van den Bruck's conserva-
tive-revolutionary ideology there is no echo in the dramas. In fact,
Barlach found *Das dritte Reich* (1923) unreadable. "He has written well on Italy and Prussian style. But his book *The Third Reich*

I can't read. It's immature, sophomoric," commented Barlach to his friend Piper.[9] His relationship with Däubler was a close personal one, and to judge by his correspondence, Barlach read Däubler's *Nordlicht*. One is tempted to look for evidence of an intellectual and literary dialogue between the two, a parallel to the Goethe-Schiller exchange. Actually, nothing of the sort took place, though Däubler wrote an essay on Barlach's sculpture and Barlach commented at length on the figure of Däubler in letters, diaries, and in the autobiographical novel *Seespeck*.

It was the nonliterary Däubler, Däubler the man, the gluttonous preacher of crystalline spirituality, who occupied Barlach. *Das Nordlicht* had for him no worth other than what it revealed about its author. In the fragmentary sketches "Diario Däubler," "Gesprächsphantasie," and in the notes for a drama entitled "Der Jüngste Tag" Barlach tries to extract the essence of Däubler and of his relationship to him.[10] These detailed notations reveal far more about the genesis of a Barlach drama than would a careful study of all possible literary sources. They are, in fact, set down as sources for later dramas. The conflict or juxtaposition *"Däubler and I"* can be seen in the basic dramatic situation of a number of Barlach's plays.[11] Yet there is no single figure in any drama which can be clearly identified as Däubler. His attributes are combined with those of others of a quite different character such as the ascetic misanthropic Albert Kollmann, who also was subjected to Barlach's scrutiny for later use.[12] The models for Barlach's characters do not come from books; they might once have been found in Wedel, Berlin, or on the streets of Güstrow. He remarked once to Reinhard Piper, "In Stuttgart they made a mystery play out of my *Der blaue Boll*, I have been told. They stylized my Boll as a simple peasant. That is naturally altogether wrong. He is a rather alcoholic squire. I see him drive by my window every morning." [13] And from the same source we find recorded, "See that girl there who is propelling herself in her wheelchair? We have three ladies like that in Güstrow, and I have observed all three carefully. One of them is Sabine in my *Sedemunds*. Yes, people in Güstrow know all about [the models for my characters]." [14]

Likewise, the events of his dramas are often dictated by the specific background before which they take place, rather than by any literary source. For instance, Barlach could not imagine a production of *Die echten Sedemunds* which did not have an exact replica of the burial vault in Güstrow known as the *Katharinengruft* (scene 5). Further examples would be the architectural plan of the inn at Lüttenbargen in *Der arme Vetter* or the tower and interior of the Cathedral in *Der blaue Boll*. At the age of nineteen, Barlach had been inspired by his reading of James Fenimore Cooper to write an Indian novel, whereby he used the following procedure: "I sketched the plan of a landscape. . . . Then I began to devise for each reference point an interesting episode that was especially suited to the locale and depended on the nature of the locale. Finally I fitted together the results achieved, I forged my novel from many pieces into a solid whole . . . but seldom finished it completely." [15] Many of his plays composed thirty and more years later seem the product of a like technique.

In short, the writings of other authors gave Barlach little beyond confirmation of his own ideas or, in the case of his first published drama, *Der tote Tag*, a shocked ex post facto awareness of psychoanalytical implications. In 1916, Dr. Julius Cohen sent him what must have been a detailed Freudian interpretation of *Der tote Tag* and received a long letter in reply. In it Barlach denies any concern with the sex instinct and psychoanalytical theory. However, the play continued to attract attention and later received the Jungian treatment at the hands of Erich Neumann in his *Ursprungsgeschichte des Bewußtseins*. Neumann writes, "The mother has killed his [her son's] horse and so castrated her son. There came a dead day, a day without sun. His denial of fathergod, identical with self-mutilation, ends in suicide. The mother's curse, counteracted by no paternal blessing, is fulfilled. He obeys the mother who bore him and he dies by her curse. An accursed mother's son.

"This drama is a myth of early times." [16]

Barlach answered Dr. Cohen, "I am everywhere and always too much a mystic, . . . the only true drive to transcend oneself is for me no reaction that can be produced by the sex instinct, I reckon my origins not from behind, . . . but rather from ahead and above." [17]

II Der arme Vetter: *Sources and Parallels*

If one looks closely at Barlach's second drama, *Der arme Vetter,* one notes that the transformation of living persons into stage characters is no simple process. Of the two central male figures, one, Siebenmark, might be recognized as Barlach's "ego" in bourgeois costume. The other, Hans Iver, embodies traits of Däubler and Kollmann, and he speaks occasionally for the author. Cautious as this may sound, it is still a rude oversimplification based only on what has been published of Barlach's papers.

Looking further in *Der arme Vetter* for parallels and evidence of sources, one comes first to the Bible. Easter and the theme of resurrection lie at the center of the action. To be sure, the events of the play bear only a slight resemblance to the Passion story; in fact, they seem to point out that the old fable is too simple, if not absurd. Such was Barlach's stated aim a few years later in writing *Die Sündflut,* namely to revise the story of the Flood, which he did in a serious, if not piously dogmatic, way. Elsewhere Biblical elements are easy to discern. The figure, or statue, of Christ is important in *Die echten Sedemunds;* old Sedemund talks to it before he marches at the head of the "Höllenbrüder." One main character is crucified; it is, however, a pregnant woman, Celestine, in *Die gute Zeit.* Finally, Barlach does not hesitate to bring God onto the stage in all too human guise. As the ineffectual wanderer in *Die Sündflut,* he is the forerunner of Wolfgang Borchert's "old man in whom no one believes any longer" in *Draußen von der Tür* (1947) and of the absurdly comic Chinese deities in Brecht's *Good Woman of Setzuan* (1943).

Despite the consistent distortion of traditional Biblical and Christian motifs, it is obvious that Barlach aims not to negate but to show them in a new light. Actually, *Der arme Vetter* and most other Barlach plays have many points in common with medieval mystery plays. Not the least of these are irreverence—quite conscious on Barlach's part—and crass juxtaposition of sacred and profane elements. Hofmannsthal tried to recreate medieval religious drama by means of adaptation. On the other hand, to judge by his pejorative use of the word "mysteries," [18] Barlach was not familiar with religious plays like the *Redentin Easter Play* (1464); and yet his dramas are closer to them in spirit than most other modern mysteries. Paul Böckmann's characterization of the medieval religious stage applies equally well to Barlach's best plays: "The closer the event of redemption is brought to personal experience, the more palpably aware the audience becomes that it calls all earthly, wordly actions into question. The event of redemption and the earthly event must threaten more and more to cancel each other out; viewed from the standpoint of the one, the other must appear as madness and folly. . . . In this dialectic lies the basis for the juxtaposition of spiritual mysticism and drastic realism in the late Middle Ages, but also for the combining of sacred and worldly action in religious drama." [19]

Accordingly, in *Der arme Vetter* one might ask which is the greater fool, Hans Iver (Christ) or his tormentor, the veterinarian costumed as Frau Venus. Iver's martyrdom resembles the traditional mocking of Christ as fool, but Barlach's figure, in turn, ridicules his persecutors. More significant than this and other parallels is the distinction between *Der arme Vetter* and the early mysteries. In the medieval Easter play, Christ is the king of fools up to the point of His resurrection, whereupon the folly is seen to be all on the worldly side. In Barlach's drama, however, though he is enjoined to do so, Iver does not rise again; and the process, in which spiritual and worldly forces threaten to cancel each other out, simply continues. The double satire on the two realms is ended arbitrarily by the dropping of the curtain. This standoff and the open end are perhaps the Protestant counterpart to Claudel's happy miracles (*The Tidings Brought to Mary*), Hofmannsthal's reverence for his sources, or the uneasy fiction of the children's king in *Der Turm* (*The Tower*).

At least two other completed dramas by Barlach may be classified as mysteries. *Der Findling* reminds one of a Christmas play; and *Die gute Zeit* is clearly a Passion play dominated by the emblem of the Cross. In addition, the "Teufelspiel"—the independent devil scenes of the medieval Easter play—finds counterparts in the mad procession of "brothers in hell" in *Die echten Sedemunds* and in the tavern scenes of *Der arme Vetter* and *Der blaue Boll.*

In all these parallels, Barlach's delight in contradiction and contrast shines forth. The hellish brotherhood starts its parade in a cathedral. The second barroom scene (6) in *Der arme Vetter* is devil play and mocking of Christ at the same time. In *Der blaue Boll*, Elias maintains his bar—"The Cozy Devil's Kitchen"—directly across the street from the Apostolic Community.[20] *Faust* has its share of devil scenes; it also depends on sharp contrast and abrupt transition. Yet Goethe and the mysteries keep heaven and hell reasonably distinct. Barlach, on the other hand, aims for the effect of grotesque incongruity by erasing distinctions and mixing one with the other.

Themes and motifs reminiscent of *Faust* haunt several of Barlach's dramas, and the temptation to indulge in parallel hunting is hard to resist.[21] But the ground is treacherous and the quarry elusive. His Gretchen figure—Grete Grüntal in *Der blaue Boll*—is the half insane wife of a swineherd and mother of three children. She is not seduced but rather brazenly offers her favors to Boll in exchange for poison to kill her children. Although they share the motifs of seduction, poison, infanticide, and dissatisfaction with the status quo, the two dramas have little in common. Likewise, the cosmic frame of *Die Sündflut* has reminded critics of the "Prolog in Heaven," but again the connection is tenuous. Barlach's Lord is a traveler and later a cripple; and his angels' hymn of praise becomes a parody of itself with the second or third repetition.

To return to *Der arme Vetter*, here, too, we find outlines that might be the residue of a study of *Faust*. The opening scenes are an "Easter Holiday" constructed like Goethe's garden scene. Two couples appear alternately on the stage. One is an engaged pair about to separate forever; the other two are Frau Keferstein and Sailor Bolz, whom no convention or inhibition can restrain from impromptu intercourse in the dunes. Also, the barren landscape in the heath along the upper Elbe, like the characters who move about in it, stands in harsh contrast to Goethe's cultivated, middle-class garden.

Any development of a love story like the Gretchen episode is effectively blocked by the intrusion of a Werther figure, Hans Iver, at the beginning. In fact, by shooting himself in scene 2 he drives the decisive wedge between the engaged pair. Barlach's triangle has no obvious counterpart in literature except possibly that of Werther, Lotte, and Albert. Although it is no *Werther* parody, *Der arme Vetter* does turn the novel's action topsy-turvy. For

by shooting himself and then dying slowly before a large public;
Iver wins the prize: Fräulein Isenbarn renounces her fiancé in
favor of Iver's corpse. Also, Iver is quite unsentimental and often
sarcastic. He has no interest in nature. Rather, it is his fellow men
who become for him "a monster that perpetually devours, forever
ruminates." [22]

His comments on their wolfish, blood-sucking nature are reminiscent of werewolf legends, whence his name comes. "Hans
Iwer" is the title of a ballad by Claus Groth (1819–99). Groth was
Barlach's favorite Low-German poet, and the poem must have
been in his mind when he wrote *Der arme Vetter*. It tells how the
farmer Hans Iwer, transformed into a werewolf, finds release in
death when his milkmaid calls him by name. Name calling and
the question of identity are important motifs in Barlach's drama,
but his Hans Iver is not redeemed by anyone. Nor is it he who is
the monster, but rather the hungry thirsty guests at the inn, who
lust after his flesh and blood.

On the other hand, Barlach's Iver is closely related to vampire
figures of the nineteenth-century *Weltschmerz* tradition, who are
condemned to wander as revenants until they are released, perhaps by the devotion of a woman. Like Lenau's Ahasver, he
moves about without purpose and feels himself a prisoner in
jail.[23] He searches in vain for his death. Even a bullet in his
breast seems to have no effect. Like a Lenau figure, again, he
wanders across the heath and suffers from a wound—in Barlach
no longer metaphorical—in his bosom. His beloved, like Lenau's,
is a pure, exalted, inaccessible being. Yet all these parallels do not
lead far, for Barlach's Iver wants neither love nor outside help. He
may choose to walk along the shore, but for him it is not a place
for declicious sentimental reverie or for indulging his feelings of
despair. Rather, he goes there to meet his antagonist and complete his act of suicide. His *Weltschmerz*, or "Ichschmerz," is an
ambiguous matter. It takes the form of abhorrence of the flesh,
but he admits he is no ascetic and enjoys his grog with the others.
Similarly, Grete Grüntal in *Der blaue Boll* says repeatedly, "Away
with flesh," but tries at the same time to seduce Boll.

Repeated allusions to Richard Wagner in *Der arme Vetter*—
e.g., "Walkyrie," "Prayer from Lohengrin," "Frau Venus"—invite
a comparison of Iver with the *Weltschmerz* hero of *The Flying*

Dutchman. Both are misanthropes and yearn for death. An earthly marriage is for both unthinkable; they think only in terms of the beyond. Fräulein Isenbarn's pledge to be true to Iver comes, however, after his death; it is offered on her own initiative and not in response to any plea. In fact, the two are no more than chance acquaintances. Also, the references to *Lohengrin* are tempting bait but lead to a maze of vague, elusive similarities.[24]

A more concrete connection with Wagner may be seen in the common interest in alliteration, or in Germanic *Stabreim*. In his *Ring* libretto, Wagner uses an alliterative pattern like the one he found in the Norse *Eddas*. On the other hand, Barlach's alliterative passages betray no system. They are evidence of his inclination to play with language and sound. For Wagner, in contrast, it is a sensual device to combine the expression of one emotion with that of another and to insinuate the connection as a natural one on the listener's ear. He writes: "The capacity of the directly receptive ear is so unlimited in this regard that it can combine sensations that are at the farthest remove from each other as soon as they are presented to it with similar physiognomies. It then transmits them to the emotions where they are embraced and absorbed as closely related, purely human sensations. What is the naked intellect when matched against this all-embracing, all-combining, miraculous power of the sense organ!"[25]

Barlach uses alliteration in the same way, that is, to make connections between things usually thought of as distinct. But he is not dealing with the same emotions, nor does he try to lull the ear into acceptance of the connection. Barlach's alliteration has an immediate irritating, even confusing effect on the listener. The alliterative leitmotivs used in *Der blaue Boll* and, particularly, in *Die Sündflut* are designed to awaken the audience's critical capacity and to throw into question one or both of the disparate elements brought together by their similar sound.

III *Grotesque Comedy and Jean Paul*

Barlach takes neither *Weltschmerz* nor alliteration as seriously as does Wagner. Nothing is more alien to him than Wagnerian pathos. The one aspect of nineteenth-century literature which occupied him throughout his life was the grotesque-comic tradition he saw represented in Jean Paul, Dickens, Gottfried Keller, and in one contemporary, Alfred Kubin. Of dramatists in the same tradition, such as Tieck, Grabbe, Büchner, Wedekind, there is no mention in Barlach's published writings. Yet, though he seems to have isolated himself, this time from the influence of others in the genre he cultivated, Barlach wrote dramas which fit neatly into the open form pattern presented by Volker Klotz.[26] Similarly, Barlach is included in the tradition of the grotesque theater Klaus Völker traces from Lenz, Grabbe, and Büchner through to Brecht and Ionesco.[27] Such traits as the law of crass contrast, the hero as fool, plays on words, the near absence of psychology, and even such seemingly trivial items as macabre tavern scenes and satirical names are all to be found in Barlach's *Der arme Vetter, Die echten Sedemunds,* and *Der blaue Boll.*

Völker maintains that Jean Paul (1763–1825) was the first to make the grotesque a legitimate esthetic category; and it is to this novelist, rather than the grotesque playwrights, that Barlach felt most drawn. Although they seem quite dissimilar at first glance, the reading of Jean Paul's novels left its mark on Barlach's dramas and, most clearly, on the unfinished novel, *Der gestohlene Mond.*

Aside from the predilection for small-town, middle-class backgrounds, it is the choice of names and the playing with identities which link Barlach most obviously with Jean Paul. By calling the two main characters in his novel Wau and Wahl, Barlach points unmistakably to the brothers Walt and Vult in *Die Flegeljahre* (*The Awkward Years*) as his models. However, little of Jean Paul's sentimentalism is to be found in the demonic dominion of Wahl over Wau; nor is there any prospect that saintly simplicity will triumph over the world.

The use of suggestive or comic names is practised by several prose realists of the nineteenth century, among them Freytag, Raabe, Keller, and, later, Thomas Mann. Barlach was familiar with most, if not all, of these. Yet he stands closer to Jean Paul than to any of the others. Both choose names which seem to suggest much but which are seldom specifically descriptive. The effect of their sound is often more important than their allegorical meaning. The cast of almost any Barlach play offers examples such as the morticians Gierhahn und Ehrbahn, Schaukelstrick, Kutscher Karl, Wandervogel Susemihl, Kapitän Pickenpack, Uhrmacher Virgin, and Frau Unk. Some names, like Siebenmark or Hans Iver, seem at first to characterize their bearers but later prove ambiguous. The end effect is purposely created confusion.[28]

Both Barlach and Jean Paul belong to a kind of underground German literary tradition that begins with the rise of individualism and self-expression in the later eighteenth century. These writers—Johann Georg Hamann, Jean Paul, Stifter in his early works, Keller, Raabe, and Barlach, among others—are seldom members of schools or easily linked to groups. They go their way often in defiance of contemporary modes. They live in isolation and cultivate their personal and literary idiosyncrasies. Their style is drastically original and their humor more grotesque than gentle.

Barlach and Jean Paul view this world as an ill-ventilated narrow pass. Their works consist of a peculiar mixture of idealism, deep meaning, disgust, and laughter. The human condition is bemoaned and ridiculed because it is seen under the aspect of eternity. In the foreground stand the human body—for them a ludicrous lump of flesh—and a dizzying multiplicity of things. But in the background one sees the timeless horizon and the ethereal beauty of sunsets.

Both authors move with confusing speed from concretion to abstraction. The ideal and real worlds collide repeatedly in what seems at first an effort to strike a balance and find a single perspective from which to view both with calm. This viewpoint, on the few occasions it is reached, is soon lost again. It is, for Jean Paul and Barlach, the movement itself that counts, so that their works never come to a satisfactory conclusion.

One sees the principle of disconcerting movement and unresolved conflict in the close relationship between sentimental characters and cynical all-seeing humorists. Both find themselves hanging somewhere between heaven and the grave. One sees it in Jean Paul, where the elaborate metaphors lead away from the thread of narrative and in Barlach where the sound and context of words contradict the literal meaning.

This double vision emerges most strikingly in the problem of personal identity that occupies both authors. Squire Boll in *Der blaue Boll,* for instance, again and again disconcerts his wife and the audience by speaking of himself in the third person. "Everyone's his own best neighbor"—"Jeder ist sich selbst der Nächste"

—runs through the play as a leitmotif and is amplified by phrases like "Boll has Boll by the collar" and "Boll is killing Boll." [29]

Jean Paul even has a figure with three names, or three characters of identical appearance, depending on how one looks at it. Parallels to this character, named Schoppe, Leibgeber, or Siebenkäs, to the cabinet of wax figures, and to the room of mirrors in Jean Paul's *Titan* can be discerned also in Barlach's *Der arme Vetter*. There, Hans Iver, like Schoppe, is obsessed by mirrors. He changes his identity and past at will. The dummy stuffed with cork and named "handsome Emil" serves, like Jean Paul's wax figures, to suggest "the utter insignificance of the body" or "the confusing alien nature of the body." [30]

In Jean Paul's novel and in *Der arme Vetter,* this confrontation with the specter of one's own body in mirrors and dummies, be it comic or serious, erases the borderline between spook and reality and destroys all naive assurance about body, self, and world. Max Kommerell writes of Jean Paul's humor with reference to the novel *Siebenkäs,* "Thus the humor strides forward in self-discovery: the discordance between soul and world becomes discordance between the ego and its corporeal form, then between the mind and the ego." [31] Barlach's Iver, the poor relation, and—to an extent—his antagonist, Siebenmark, follow the same path. Iver views the world as a trap, cannot bear the sight of himself in the mirror, and chooses suicide in preference to living with himself.

Jean Paul's Siebenkäs runs away from the uncomfortable bonds of job, small town, and marriage. Iver, on the other hand, is motivated by a radical, metaphysical disgust with himself and all about him. He has little humor. Barlach's humor arises from the juxtaposition of Iver's world-disgust and the opposite, purely animal extreme. The wit is to be found in the crude characters who ridicule him. Thus Barlach casts doubt on Iver's position and, unlike Jean Paul, clearly gives the world its due. He presents crasser contrasts and places his central figure, Siebenmark, in the crossfire between the two opposing forces. Siebenmark then finds his proper place "between earth and heaven," whereas Jean Paul's heroes continue to aim for the stars.

A comparison of the diction of the two authors offers much the same picture. Jean Paul chafes under the limitations imposed by words and syntax just as Siebenkäs abhors all earthly encumbrance. Language becomes a device for demonstrating the superiority of the infinite over the finite.[32] This tendency toward abstraction is equally strong in Barlach, particularly in the figure of Iver, whose speeches are sometimes pure allegory. Barlach's plays are filled, as are Jean Paul's novels, with concrete details, but they are not used to demonstrate the victory of mind over matter. Barlach's realism works to counter the tendency to fly off to the stars. Crude language about worldly matters is carefully designed to make mystical speculation seem ridiculous or at least to encourage second thoughts on the matter. Further fruitful bases of comparison, such as the figure of the devil, suggest themselves, for the imprint of Jean Paul on Barlach's work is deeper than that of any other writer. Yet what happens to the source in the assimilative process is the same transformation we have already repeatedly observed. Traces of the original are left, but the effect is nearly the reverse.

IV Jugendstil

The danger of abstraction, of losing oneself in the stars, was one which Barlach recognized in himself and which he presented in the characterization of Hans Iver. In fact, *Der arme Vetter* marks the point in his literary career when this danger is overcome. His earlier writings from the time, say, before 1906 are best characterized as *Jugendstil*. They sometimes have a Jean Paul-like whimsy, but the style is flat and allegorical. Like his drawings from the same time, they lack depth perspective.

Volker Klotz's remarks on a poem by Stadler could apply equally well to some early Barlach prose pieces: ". . . sultry, tangled scenery with selected props and furnished with pretentious adjectives, which despite its animation can scarcely breathe." [33] To judge by passages from occasional writings of the time after 1906 and by *Der arme Vetter,* the transition from *Jugendstil* to Barlach's mature style was a memorable event. The word "stylization," which best describes his early treatment of landscapes and persons, is used in later years in a purely pejorative sense. The development of Barlach's style shows a turning away from artificial constructions to the everyday world. The process is repeated in the conflicts and resolutions of his plays. The artificial ethereal atmosphere of the opening scenes in *Die gute Zeit,* for instance, is evoked in order to be ridiculed and as a contrast to the earthiness of the bad time and the humanity of the crucified heroine in between. Rather than reconcile and fuse contradictions, as *Jugendstil* seeks to do, Barlach seeks more and more to sharpen them. Human figures are not seen as part of the landscape but rather in distinct contrast to it as, for example, when Fräulein Isenbarn utters a joyous welcome to Easter on the barren heath in *Der arme Vetter.*

There are several *Jugendstil* motifs in the latter drama, and most of them are intensified or distorted. The mystical contemplation of the unity of time and eternity, or individual and all, becomes transformed in Iver into a frenetic flight from time and self. Rebirth and transfiguration of the body become in him abhorrence of the flesh and suicide.[34] Something of the basic situation in *Der arme Vetter* is suggested in Dolf Sternberger's statement about *Jugendstil:* "The idea of *Jugendstil* was to surround persons and even the whole epoch with nothing but reflections of their own inwardness, to envelop them in this ring and dance of forms. Narcissus died because he had lost himself to his own mirror image."[35] In the play, however, the main characters are painfully aware that they are surrounded by mirrors and try to break out in one way or another.

Of all the play's characters, Fräulein Isenbarn bears the closest resemblance to a stock *Jugendstil* figure, namely the madonna. In her state of blissful transport she is unconcerned with concepts such as flesh and sin. Yet, as in Iver's case, Barlach gives the motif a grotesque twist. She is stripped of erotic qualities; and rather than become "the pure helpmeet who does not disturb her man, . . . but walks in radiance at his side forever onward and upward," she turns into a sort of Valkyrie and goes her way alone.[36] She declares this independence by a kiss—another *Jugendstil* motif ever present in Rodin's statue. Barlachian distortion makes it a kiss of death. By kissing Iver's corpse, she severs herself from all that her fiancé, and perhaps a writer like Richard Dehmel, understands by "life."[37] She is best compared with the cool, distant aspect of a star.

The images of star, flame, and crystal, common allegorical emblems among theosophists and *Jugendstil* writers at the turn of the century and after, are all important in *Der arme Vetter*. In Barlach, however, they are no longer unambiguous symbols of transfiguration and spiritualization. The flame, for instance, appears as a smoky guttering oil lamp.[38] It goes out twice at crucial points in the play, the second time when Fräulein Isenbarn renounces the world and opts in favor of the stars. She experiences, and tries to describe, what might be called, after a phrase from Jakob Böhme's *Aurora*, a sidereal birth.[39]

Siderische Geburt is the title of a book which appeared in 1910 (Berlin: Karl Schnabel). Its author uses the penname of Volker. Barlach read it in February and March, 1913, and it intoxicated him. Thereafter there is but one possible reference to it in his published writings: a quotation taken from a friend's letter.[40] Yet he is said to have read the book repeatedly and to have made marginal notations. Horst Wagner draws attention to it and claims it to be an important source for Barlach's ideas and a model for his diction.[41] As the title and subtitle ("Seraphische Wanderung vom Tode der Welt zur Taufe der Tat" [Seraphic Wandering from the Death of the World to the Baptism of the Deed]) indicate, the contents are a strange mixture of Nietzschean cultural criticism, Jakob Böhme, theosophy, and apocalyptic prophecy presented in quite un-Barlachian, erotically colored, florid prose which speaks often of "grenzenlose Umarmung" and "seliges Schwingen und Schweben im Außer-sich-Seyn" (limitless close embrace and blissful swinging and swaying in a state of ecstasy).

The use of alliteration in the text is negligible, but there are a few phrases, particularly in the chapter "The World Beneath Me," which are analogous to formulations in later Barlach dramas. The sentence, "Our time is end and beginning of everything, is the Easter resurrection of the godhead from its wintery prison," could well have been in Barlach's mind when he wrote speeches for Fräulein Isenbarn in *Der arme Vetter*. Also, the description of this world as the realm of confinement, gluttony, and sensuality ("Enge, Fraß und Tast"—p. 199) and of mirrors (p. 25) is echoed in several plays.

The search for ideas which Barlach might have absorbed from Volker is complicated by the preacherly tone of *Siderische Geburt*. One statement, for example: "He who will not experience the world's autumnal withering, . . . cannot be reborn in the sacred spring" (p. 12), at best paraphrases in a pale vague way the moral of *Die Sündflut* and perhaps *Der blaue Boll.* More telling are the radical differences between Barlach and Volker. The latter's seraphic lyricism, his "swinging and swaying," are clearly *Jugendstil* as is also his harmonious, cyclical world-process free of all dialectical contradiction. He considers himself a metaphysician and scorns the materially minded. Ethics are not his concern. He has an easy solution to the problem of evil; his system simply makes it unimportant. In all these matters he is the antithesis of Barlach.

The sources which Barlach used to formulate his world view may well include *Siderische Geburt,* but it is less important than Volker's own source: Jakob Böhme.[42] Meister Eckhart, Chinese poet-philosophers, nineteenth-century social Christianity as represented by Charles Kingsley,[43] and Nietzsche, uncongenial as they may seem, also left their mark. In Kingsley Barlach found his own concern for social responsibility and the theodicy problem; in Nietzsche his anti-bourgeois iconoclasm; from Meister Eckhart he appropriated some elements of mystical vocabulary, especially in the last pages of *Die Sündflut;* from Böhme, sooner than Volker, are drawn images of mirror, crystal, light, and flame. The proximity to Böhme is revealed also in Barlach's Protestant mystical visions—in his own experience and in writings such as *Der gestohlene Mond*—, the adventurous use of language, and above all the tension and contradiction between strong ties to this world and allegiance to an ascetic faith.

Here, as in matters of purely literary sources and technique, Barlach shows consistent fidelity to no single tradition. The absorption of Kingsley and Nietzsche, altogether antithetical figures, into his thought is a striking instance of his eclectic elasticity. In an attempt to break his work down into components possibly borrowed one finds, first, parallels to nineteenth-century figures like Wagner and Jean Paul, to the comic-grotesque tradition, and religious thought of the era. But the roots reach deeper, back to Böhme and the Baroque, the Passion play and the mystics, and beyond to Lao Tse. Barlach seemingly tries to maintain his isolation and independence by pairing disparate conflicting elements which work to unmask each other. In *Die echten Sedemunds,* analogously, an idealistic Adamist son clashes with his bourgeois sensual father. Once "the lion is loose," the hypocrisy of both is laid bare. Barlach's reverence for the past is paired with caustic scepticism. In a letter written in 1915 he remarks, "I know I will have Goethe with me as long as I keep going." A few years later, however, he says of Goethe in a conversation, "Schiller is heroic, Goethe isn't. He lacks tragic dignity. There is no doom. A rosy old man revolts me." [44]

His relationship to the expressionist school of drama is also characterized by contradictions. The voluntary exile from Berlin and the diatribes against the expressionist theater do not disguise the fact that he wanted his plays performed under the great directors of the time and that he had much in common with the playwrights he avoided. The similarity is limited largely to themes such as father-son, lord-servant relationships and the idea of transformation. Theater people mistook the distant kinship for identity and produced his plays as they did those of Georg Kaiser and lesser figures of the "dawn-of-humanity" persuasion. Despite earnest effort, such productions usually failed, for directors did not see that Barlach gave the themes a new content quite different from current clichés about class struggle, war of generations, and the new man. They also failed to see that Barlach's work represented the transition from expressionism to the theater of today precisely because it was not modern in their sense. His affinities to the nineteenth century and to the medieval stage demanded a style of production both realistic and visionary, crude and refined.

An exhaustive study of all "Barlach and . . ." possibilities is a desperately hard task.[45] His borrowings, if they can be called that, are highly eclectic, and many parallels must be considered accidental. Barlach apparently never turned to tradition in search of material or models. What he sought was rather confirmation, and he was pleased to find something of which he could say, as he did of Lao Tse and other Chinese poets, "It teems with Barlachdom in my sense." [46]

CHAPTER 7

Theatrical Fortunes and Misfortunes

A MORE accurate title for this chapter might have been "Barlach versus the Theater" or better "The Theater versus Barlach," for there was never any proper reciprocal relationship between them.[1] In his lifetime there was, to put it mildly, misunderstanding on both sides, and since the war some of the tension has lived on in the attitudes of theater people and critics.

The question of whether Barlach's dramas deserve a place in the repertoire of major theaters or are best played occasionally on a studio stage still has to be answered and can be answered only in practice. The most a discussion like this can do is to sketch the stage history of the four best plays and draw theoretical conclusions about reasons for theatrical success or failure.

The so-called Barlach renaissance in leading German theaters during the early and middle 1950's has miscarried; and, in general, the attempts in recent years to recapture his work for the stage have led only to *succès d'estime* and short runs. During Barlach's lifetime and even during the theatrical golden age of the 1920's, it was little different. In those years, many reviewers recognized him as the strongest dramatist of the age. A few others thought quite the opposite; Alfred Kerr, who judged each work by purely theatrical and subjective critieria, classified him among "the little flops of the postwar era" cowering in convulsive impotence and full of hot air.[2]

Barlach's personal experience and his utterances on the topic offer a good picture in miniature of the tangled problem. Probably no dramatist has ever felt himself more mistreated and misunderstood by directors and audiences, and few have done less to correct the situation. He betrays his uneasiness in a letter written in 1919 dealing with the imminent *première* of his first published drama, *Der tote Tag*: "To see to it that my conviction is conveyed to others is a task incumbent on the presentation, but the question is whether that which moved me can be conveyed at all." [3] Thus before his first *première* Barlach is troubled with doubts about the dramaturgical adequacy of his play and, more important, about the alien spectator, who, he fears, will not understand it.

Later, once he had arrived as a writer, he ceased to worry about the problems of communication and placed the blame for poor reception of his work on directors and a lazy recalcitrant audience. Unlike Bertolt Brecht, he took no measures to intrigue or activate his audience, nor did he consider making revisions for dramaturgical reasons. In another letter, written also in 1919, he speaks of his disinclination even to adapt dramas in progress to the requirements of the stage: "But I have too little stage experience and am altogether too little bent on the theater to infer or gain anything from a performance." [4]

Later Barlach accepted, even affirmed and sharpened, his alienation from the theater and contented himself with occasional caustic comments from his isolation in Güstrow. Even the possibility that the renowned Max Reinhardt might produce *Die echten Sedemunds* in Berlin failed to excite him, if one is to believe the letter to Karl Barlach, his cousin, written on July 10, 1920: "After all, for me this final stunt can scarcely be a part of the work, a bit of 'illusory life after death,' a bit of ghosting and spooking by a deceased friend." [5]

On a few occasions, however, Barlach did let himself become involved in the staging of his plays. In each instance he soon regretted it and withdrew altogether. He could not block all avenues of approach but did his best to discourage attempts to get his advice. In 1926, for example, Edzard Schaper, then an assistant director at the Stuttgart Landestheater, came to Güstrow to discuss Barlach's latest play, *Der blaue Boll*. Stuttgart was to be the scene of the world *première*, as it had been, two years earlier, for *Die Sündflut*. Apprised of the visit's purpose, Barlach asked Schaper whether he had read the play. Schaper admitted he hadn't. Thereupon Barlach bought him a copy and abandoned him in Güstrow's Hotel Erbgroßherzog for the rest of the day. That evening they met again, and Barlach asked once more if he had read the play. Schaper replied that he had read and understood everything. "Marvelous, then we don't need to say another

word about it," said Barlach. Schaper then had to content himself
with an extended evening over grog in the *Erbgroßherzog*.[6]

Schaper was not the first to suffer this brusque treatment and
was perhaps aware that theater people had become scapegoats for
Barlach's dismay at the fate of his dramas on the stage. To be
sure, the alien audience remained unchanged, as Barlach indicates
in a letter (1927) dealing with productions of his *Die Sündflut:*
"No trace of effectiveness, the people feel insulted by such demands on their thinking capacity." The letter then waxes hotter
and reveals the real sore point: ". . . and moreover, what devil
rides those theater directors that they all want to make oratorios
and medieval mysteries out of my dramas instead of entertaining
pieces!" [7] Barlach does not stop with directors but goes on, in the
succeeding lines, to vent his rage on costume and stage designers
who seemingly aim to make his plays as boring as possible—in
most cases by basing their designs on his sculpture and drawings.
Barlach was convinced, with good reason, that his plastic and dramatic work were separate entities and could not be synthesized
without destroying the effect of each.

I *The Case of* Die echten Sedemunds

This letter is but one of several utterances preserved from the
1920's. In them one incident stands out: It is the first important
production of a Barlach play in the theater capital, Leopold
Jeßner's staging of *Die echten Sedemunds* in the Berlin Staatstheater on April 1, 1921. In that year Jeßner was out to discover
new dramatists who would provide material for performance on
the steps of his revolutionary, abstract stage. He chose Carl Zuck-
mayer and Barlach. Neither was well received, because their plays
were too concrete to fit the surroundings. Jeßner visited Güstrow
to discuss plans for the production, and Barlach, despite himself,
was enthusiastic about the visit and the prospect of a good professional treatment of his drama. He wrote to Reinhard Piper: "Yes-
terday the director of the Berlin Staatstheater was here, something is really going to happen now with *Die echten Sedemunds*
and with all the frills in fact. . . . It is decidedly fantastic to sit
across from someone who has lived so intensively through all the
phases that one has tested out on oneself . . ." [8]

Yet as the day of the *première* drew closer, Barlach became more hesitant. A glance at Jeßner's sketches persuaded him that the production would conform more to the director's "imperious stylistic intent" than to the spirit of the text. In fact he forsaw a clash between his play—"an incidental bit of casual nonsense"— and the strait jacket Jeßner was imposing on it—"between rigidly stylized walls." The epithet "stylized" must be understood in a pejorative sense; it appears with variations like "Monumental-Stilbums" (monumental style-buffoonery) in nearly all of Barlach's diatribes against the theater.[9] Small wonder that he had to be dragged against his will to see the second performance of *Die echten Sedemunds* and that this was to be his first and last viewing of one of his dramas on the stage.

The whole affair—the quarrel with the usher about seats, the whistling in the audience, the confrontation with Jeßner at the end, and the negative reviews—must have been a traumatic experience for someone not hardened to the ways of the theater. Barlach recounted it repeatedly in letters and conversations. Stripped of embellishment, all his accounts are very much like the one recorded by Friedrich Schult: "Because of the totally false stylization which simply distorted the broad tone of my play beyond recognition, I was in a terrible situation. When Jeßner asked me how I had liked the whole thing, I had to answer: What I saw here has no longer anything to do with me!"[10] On leaving the theater Barlach commented to his companion that, had he been a paying spectator, he would perhaps have been the loudest whistler.[11]

The newspaper reviews proved Barlach's judgment to be correct. Almost all critics noted the incompatability of text and production. However, the majority put the blame on the author— Barlach speaks of an "almost unanimous rejection and in some cases derision"—and praised the stage technique. Most reviewers termed the performance a triumph by Jeßner over an impossible text unfit for the stage. Alfred Kerr pulls no punches in his review: "In the last analysis, Jeßner wrote the work. Somewhat the way an ingenious cook turns a piece of leather into a cutlet with trimmings and heavenly sauces. Barlach provided the leather, Jeßner the culinary skill."[12] Other, less splenetic critics like Siegfried Jacobsohn, Herbert Ihering, and Julius Bab came closer to Barlach's viewpoint. Bab writes: "But the entire production in its denatured, stubbornly preserved marionette style lagged behind the poetic grandeur of the text." [13]

The whistling spectators and the derisive reviews aroused a resentment in Barlach that found expression in his mockery of theater people. In 1928, long after the event, he described Jeßner's reaction to his comment ("Why, I can't recognize my own play!") on the performance as follows: "Jeßner stared at me bug-eyed, and only then did it occur to me that he most likely expected great gushing flattery from me, gushing flattery on his fabulous directorial skill. Naturally you don't make many friends that way among theater people." [14]

The destinies of Barlach's dramas on the stage fall into no distinct pattern, nor can the frequency or infrequency of their inclusion in the repertoires of German theaters be easily explained. One might ask, for instance, why *The Genuine Sedemunds,* a play with several roles appealing to actors and with more humor and stage potential than most contemporary pieces, should have been produced altogether four times from its world *première* in Hamburg (March 23, 1921) to the politically reckless Altona *mise en scène* of 1935, whose run was cut short after five performances on orders from Berlin. None of these four productions was performed on more than five evenings.

The first three productions in the early 1920's were much alike in their strict stylization and expressionistic abstraction. The consensus is that they failed because they were simply inadequate or because they worked against the text, trying to make a tasty cutlet from the piece of leather. Kurt Eggers-Kestner, however, who directed the play at the Altona Stadttheater in 1935, set out to do everything according to Barlach's dictates. He writes in retrospect with some humor: "This time Barlach had followed our enterprise with concern. At the Berlin *première,* his *Sedemunds* had turned out quite differently from what he had intended and had aroused disagreement. We were well behaved and stuck to his thought and word. The stage designer Karl Gröning had set the Altona Horticultural Commission in motion to insure that the graveyard would be genuine. When, at the end, the 'genuine Grude' danced along between the graves, no one could have the slightest doubt what it meant." [15]

The results would seem to prove the rightness of Barlach's ideas on staging. As one critic wrote of Eggers-Kestner's production of *Der blaue Boll* in 1934, he made Barlach's dream come true. Most astounding, when one recalls the critical reactions to earlier performances, is the quality of the reviews. They not only show appreciation for the work on the stage but also reveal a thorough understanding of Barlach's peculiar style. The *Sedemunds* of 1935 was a revelation, particularly for viewers like Ihering, who had seen the opposite extreme in Jeßner's Berlin production. The disappearance of expressionistic plays and performances from the stage, whether in response to Nazi edict or to a change in taste, had prepared the way for a new appreciation of Barlach. But it was too late. He had been blacklisted.

The great discovery the critics made in 1935 was that *Die echten Sedemunds* was full of concrete, sensual reality in its characters, action, and—most important—in its language. Ihering recalls the 1921 performance: "It will remain an accomplishment, although in the expressionistic period of the theater the weaknesses of the drama were played: the rhetoric and not the characters. Inchoate thoughts were rendered as rigid formulas, turbid perceptions as distinct results. The miracle of this work, however, this crabbed small-town world in its evil and elemental force, in its devilish and yet eccentric humor, emerged as a stylistic experiment." [16]

Bruno E. Werner appraises Eggers-Kestner's accomplishment in a review which belongs among the very best interpretations of Barlach to be found anywhere: "He [Eggers-Kestner] had rightly understood . . . that the problem is to make real human beings visible and that nothing is worse than to immerse Barlach plays from A to Z in a dream atmosphere. For what distinguishes Barlach from expressionism is that he presents palpable reality in his familiar, native, North German atmosphere and that this reality only occasionally becomes transparent so that behind it—but never without it—one perceives the great metaphysical forces of an unmediated psychic space." [17] If anything, Werner continues, Eggers-Kestner did not go far enough in this direction. "For the play can only be understood by the spectator if all abstraction and stylization of the characters is avoided, all trace of caricature, if we really see here North German provincials and no sort of translation into theatricality (the moment this happens the spectator no longer understands these figures and tries to find a hidden meaning behind all their words . . .)"

II *Stage Misinterpretations*

These remarks apply not only to *Die echten Sedemunds* but also to Barlach's three other great dramas: *Der arme Vetter, Die Sündflut,* and *Der blaue Boll.* Werner tells how Barlach should be played and explains why critics, audiences, and scholars have failed to understand the dramas. A few false accents or the mistaken interpretation of one role, not to mention rigid stylization, suffice seriously to distort any one of them.

The melancholy stage history of *Die Sündflut* during the 1920's is a case in point. Barlach received the Kleist Prize for this drama. Yet despite this recognition most directors thought that it deserved a good deal of editing for the theater. Of all of Barlach's plays, *Die Sündflut* has been the most popular among directors—it was produced twenty times before the hiatus of the Nazi years— and least popular with audiences. Even the Berlin production (1925) under Jürgen Fehling, noted as the finest Barlach interpreter, was dropped from the repertoire after four performances. Many others were withdrawn immediately after the *première*. Audiences accorded it either perfunctory applause or, on occasion, none at all. One reviewer attributes this silence to the religious awe inspired by the play; but evidence points rather to confusion and disappointment.

The reasons for directors' enthusiasm coincide with those for the spectators' rejection. *Die Sündflut,* with its agonized questions about God and His responsibility for evil, offered a chance to set off some rhetorical fireworks. It was repeatedly transformed into a discussion piece in pathetic ultra-expressionistic style. The text was frequently shortened and simplified in such a way that its total effect was the opposite of Barlach's clear intent. The comic-grotesque scenes depicting Noah's troubled family life were omitted in order to accentuate the theological dispute between him and Calan; and the role of fat Zebid—her evil presence on the ark dooms the whole enterprise to failure—was in some cases (Fehling's as well as others') cut completely. Noah was often played according to the Bible as a venerable patriarch and Calan as a villainous brute. Stage designs were usually abstract, and actors were dressed in sacks to resemble Barlach's sculptured figures.

This experimenting and shortening, in effect, emasculated the play. In 1925 Alfred Kerr again had occasion to pan a Barlach play with phrases like "pure dilletantism" and "immeasurably boring." He comes to the same conclusion in favor of the director as he did four years earlier: "Fehling's production was more successful than the spuriously deep misdrama." [18]

As recently as 1954, in a Darmstadt production, *Die Sündflut* suffered the same distortion. Egon Vietta, dramaturge of the Landestheater, set the tone by interpreting the play as a reflection of Heidegger's philosophy; and Gustav Rudolf Sellner followed with a performance running counter to the text. The reviews indicate that it amounted to an unconscious parody of earlier productions. The characters were "only figurines with banderoles [or comic-strip balloons] on a barren expanse." [19] About the contradiction between the text and the style of production the same critic then asks, "Why this geometry in such an ungeometrical piece. Have people lost the courage to adopt a realistic style which could also be metaphorical?" According to Heinz Beckmann, the stage setting was "nothing but an abstract embarrassment with serious whiskers, so to speak." [20] Sellner's production made a "misdrama" of *Die Sündflut* by obscuring its humor, ambiguity, and humanity. The worst distortion was in the characterization of Noah; instead of a timid, vacillating man, he appeared as a sympathetic, pious Christian, according to Beckmann.

Since the war *Die Sündflut* has, on the whole, experienced more success and longer runs. In 1946 it was performed twenty times by the company of the Hamburg Schauspielhaus, for reasons, however, which had more to do with the mood of the times than with the quality of the production. The audience understood little; but the play seemed to say something about collective guilt, and the effort was thought of as expiation or reparation for Nazi sins against Barlach and the world.[21]

Finally, the Hannover Landestheater presented the play twenty-five times in 1952, a remarkable run for any Barlach drama, particularly in a small theater. To judge from the few reports available, the *mise en scène* conformed to Barlach's own ideas. The director, Jöns Anderson, avoided any hint of pathos and emphasized the comic passages by making Noah somewhat like a North German peasant.

III *Fehling's Exemplary Productions*

A compilation of the theater's many injustices to Barlach would be repetitive and fruitless. Nevertheless, a brief reference to the stage history of *Der arme Vetter* belongs here, if only to demonstrate again the irrational pattern of failure and success. For unlike the other three great plays, it found its best stage interpretation early. Jürgen Fehling directed the drama at the Berlin Staatstheater in 1923, and this, its third, production has never been surpassed in quality. The run of eighteen performances is astounding, considering the poor reception of Jeßner's *Sedemunds* two years earlier and the failure of the first two productions of *Der arme Vetter* in Hamburg and Halle (Saale), where the first and only performance was played before a nearly empty house. In fact, the fourteen productions in German theaters after Fehling's and before 1933 were received with even less applause than was *Die Sündflut*. One can only guess at the reasons, for even directors who refrained from radical stylizing (e.g., the Karlsruhe production of 1925) saw their audiences depart in silence.

Fehling's unique success may be laid in part to an alert audience and acute reviewers. However, it was mainly the combination of the finest acting talent and Fehling's faithful, lively interpretation which made the difference. Barlach's plays make demands which cannot be satisfied by every theater. Fehling had the proper ingredients and knew how to put them together. This time he cut almost nothing, so that the performance lasted nearly four hours. He did not oversimplify the subtle relationships between the three main figures, and he gave the indispensable secondary roles their due. Most important, he struck the proper combination of reality and irreality, foreground and background, which Ihering tries to describe as follows:

These persons, as expressions of this brewing atmosphere and in turn creating this atmosphere, rooted substantially in the soil of their landscape and reaching up to the stars . . . are interwoven and interpermeated and find their deep and mysterious goal in the relationship between Siebenmark, . . . his fiancée, . . . and Hans Iver, a relationship which elevates an erotic game to the ultimate metaphor, . . . whereby the earthly element is sublimated by the divine and the divine only becomes visible through the earthly. *Der arme Vetter* is the most noble and virile drama of our time.[22]

Siegfried Jacobsohn is more specific about Fehling's accomplishment: "The vapors of the region actually press in on your breast. Out of this reality, however, rises the irreality of the clairvoyant Ernst Barlach—thanks to Fehling's omission of artificial devices, to his abandonment of all fashionable nonsense, to his respect for the subject, to his feeling for the weightlessness of detail, and to his delight in enlivening musical interludes." [23]

Two years later Fehling made serious mistakes in his direction of *Die Sündflut* but more than made up for them with his production in 1930–31 of *Der blaue Boll,* which has the same provincial North German atmosphere as *Der arme Vetter.* His *Der blaue Boll* was the second of a total of three to be staged before the war. By the late 1920's, Barlach's growing reputation as a bad risk had probably discouraged even larger theaters from further experiments with his work. The world *première* of *Der blaue Boll* in 1926 at the Stuttgart Landestheater promised no better reception for this than for any earlier drama. It was a *succès d'estime* at best, and the performance was repeated only twice. One reviewer ambiguously called it surprisingly good; another thought it amateurish and a painful experience.

Fehling's Berlin *mise en scène* had the advantage of a director, a set designer (Rochus Gliese), and a cast (Heinrich George) who were excellent craftsmen and had the experience of two Barlach productions behind them. Willy Haas's comment: "It was a tremendous impression. . . . Even today my heart beats faster when I think of that evening in the theater," [24] echoes the reviews of the time. One critic calls *Der blaue Boll* not only a piece of great literature but the best play to appear on the Berlin stage in ten years.[25] Thanks to the unsparing efforts of Jürgen Fehling, the drama remained on the repertoire through twenty-eight performances. Like one of those sudden flashes of mystical recognition Barlach speaks of, this production gave a startling insight into the stage potential of his work.

Three years later, Eggers-Kestner heeded Fehling's example in his staging of *Der blaue Boll* in Altona. Like Fehling he spared neither expense nor time. Consequently the performance was termed "the most important production that has appeared on the stages of greater Hamburg this season." [26]

The upward course of Barlach's stage fortunes in the years from 1930 to 1935 tempts one to speculate on what might have happened if Hitler had not become *Reichskanzler*. If there ever was a Barlach stage style, it was the one perfected by Fehling and Eggers-Kestner in those years. Unfortunately their accomplishment did not carry over into the postwar era. Since 1945 three major productions of *Der blaue Boll* have failed to further the cause of a Barlach renaissance for reasons indicated in the discussion of *Die Sündflut*, namely, the tendency to play it in expressionistic stylization and to overemphasize its metaphysical passages.[27] "With this ethereal conception of the role of Squire Boll, the whole drama immediately shot away like a jet of flame, upwards toward the church steeple, before it had really begun," writes Heinz Beckmann of the 1953 production in Essen.[28]

Beckmann's review is entitled *"Blauer Boll*—too soon or too late?"*, a legitimate question which brings to mind parallels between the 1920's and the 1950's. The question might be reformulated: Will Barlach win his audience again as he did earlier after a decade of grudging acceptance? At all events, in the 1920's as in the 1950's audiences and directors had no organ for Barlach's matter-of-fact yet spiritual realism. The understandable choice of the German theater to start again from the basis of its achievements of the 1920's has only proven that Barlach cannot be played *à la mode*.

These remarks apply to matters of diction as well as stage technique. Eggers-Kestner's production of *Die echten Sedemunds* brought critics to the recognition that the merit of the play rests, like all great literature, on its language. Wolf Schramm says of Eggers-Kestner in a review: "He presented it completely *on the basis of the word* and completely for the sake of the word," [29] and Ihering writes of the text: "Ernst Barlach restores sensuousness to our language." [30] And finally, Günther Mann presented on this occasion an uncommonly acute description of the power of Barlach's diction: "The Barlachian world of words can after all have no 'pleasing' effect whatsoever: one is attacked by it, buffeted, metaphysically goaded into a fight, so to speak—without really knowing at first what is at stake. It is as if the everyday actions and words of the Barlachian figures suddenly burst: with one stroke, another more essential world shines through, *momentarily* —but it has caught us by surprise and makes us disconcerted." [31]

In the ensuing thirty years, no production of a Barlach play has placed the same stress on diction or received such glowing reviews. Striking stage effects have obscured the power of his language or have distracted attention from inadequate delivery of lines. Geometrical sets, exotic costumes, choreographically prescribed gestures, in short all the tricks of the stage trade have only hurt Barlach's reputation as a writer for the theater. For it is his diction which places him above his contemporaries. Paul Fechter writes in this regard: "It is Barlach who, after Wedekind, almost single-handedly has continued to carry forward the drama's controversy with the word as material and as fundamental formal element and, therewith, the problem of the renovation of inner dramatic structure." [32]

Barlach was aware, and so were Fehling and Eggers-Kestner, that unless his lines were spoken in a natural unpretentious way and unless the *mise en scène* was straightforward and realistic, his plays would shoot off toward the stars and never return. He wrote his best pieces in such a way that there would be a fine balance between reality and metaphor. Ideally a director should maintain the balance in every aspect of his production: language, gesture, and stage design. If he succeeds, the audience will have the experience described by Günther Mann: "Even though one has felt oneself at the beginning of the play to be groping as in a mysterious twilight state, in retrospect one becomes aware that one has by no means been led around in an eccentric labyrinth with unreal persons and words and that one has been guided quite meaningfully to a goal." [33]

The stylistic prejudices of directors, audiences, and critics lost their rigidity in the late 1920's. Eyes were opened to new possibilities in realism, perhaps by the power of Brecht's revolutionary productions. Around 1930 a second look at Barlach's work brought a new understanding for its peculiar use of contrast and ambiguity, which makes it both difficult and great. Expressionist fashion had made the plays seem vague and immature because it revealed only a congenial fraction of what they contained. Under Fehling and Eggers-Kestner, the whole of Barlach came to view, to the delight and astonishment of audiences and reviewers.

With Barlach, then, it is all or nothing, and the postwar theater has found it hard to satisfy his rigorous demands. The fulfillment of the following optimistic prophecy is yet to come: "In all probability people will one day understand Barlach just as easily as they understand Kleist today. Directors will then no longer stage Barlach under the influence of Strindberg, Wedekind, and Expressionism, but rather in Barlach's sense and in the spirit of a new time in which earthly realities and metaphysical reference will no longer be antitheses. The spectators will then not just applaud respectfully and loud, . . . rather they will laugh here at the comedy, be gripped by the horror . . ., and something of the great spiritual metamorphosis in this comedy [*Die echten Sedemunds*], which comes from the most profound religious perturbation, will blow over them with bold liberating force like a cool wind." [34]

Notes and References

[For abbreviations see Preface]

Chapter One

1. Ernst Barlach, *Zeichnungen aus dem Hause des Künstlers auf dem Heidberg bei Güstrow* (Hamburger Kunsthalle, 1965), p. 6.
2. *Briefe*, I, 76–77.
3. *Ibid.*, p. 64.
4. *Prosa*, I, 18.
5. *Ibid.*, p. 19.
6. *Ibid.*, p. 29.
7. *Briefe*, II, 119.
8. *Briefe*, I, 17.
9. *Briefe*, II, 58.
10. *Ibid.*, p. 178.
11. *Prosa*, I, 51.
12. *Ibid.*, p. 53.
13. *Ibid.*, p. 53–54.
14. *Briefe*, III, 22.
15. *Briefe*, II, 93.
16. *Briefe*, I, 42.
17. *Prosa*, I, 54–55.
18. *Ibid.*, p. 55.
19. *Briefe*, I, 32, 50.
20. *Prosa*, I, 241.
21. *Briefe*, I, 34.
22. *Briefe*, III, 47.
23. *Briefe*, II, 77, 75.
24. *Prosa*, II, 373–75.
25. *Briefe*, II, 64–66.
26. *Prosa*, II, 387–88.
27. *Briefe*, I, 45.
28. 1922, in *Briefe*, I, 55.
29. Reinhard Piper, *Mein Leben als Verleger* (Munich, 1964), p. 422.

30. Piper, p. 440.
31. *Briefe,* III, 121.
32. Piper, p. 436.
33. *Briefe,* III, 145.

Chapter Two

1. *Dramen*, pp. 18, 24. Parts of this chapter have appeared in *Modern Language Review*, LVII (1962), 373–84, and are here reprinted by permission of the Modern Humanities Research Association and the General Editor.

2. *Dramen*, pp. 23–24.

3. *Ibid.*, p. 54.

4. *Ibid.*, p. 95.

5. *Briefe*, II, 58, 63.

6. *General-Anzeiger für Hamburg-Altona*, March 21, 1919.

7. *Briefe*, I, 47.

8. *Briefe*, II, 83 ff.; cf. also Chapter Six, p. 107.

9. *Ibid.*, p. 94.

10. Horst Wagner's interpretation of *Die Sündflut* (*The Flood*) in Benno von Wiese, ed., *Das deutsche Drama*, 2nd ed. (Düsseldorf, 1960), II, 348.

11. *Dramen*, p. 177.

12. *Ibid.*, p. 179.

13. *Ibid.*, p. 180.

14. *Ibid.*, p. 181.

15. *Ibid.*, p. 182.

16. *Ibid.*, p. 183.

17. *Prosa*, I, 408.

18. In 1902 the steamer *Primus* went down on the Elbe with 112 passengers aboard. In *Der arme Vetter*, the crowd from the inn leaves to board a ship with the same name. Voß, Enghohm, and the three central characters stay behind. Although there is no evidence for it in the play itself, the funeral might have been that of the drowned passengers.

19. *Dramen*, p. 104. A play on words. "Do you have something on your conscience ('auf dem Gewissen')?" "On what? That certain [part of the body] ('Der Gewisse') I use to sit on."

20. A number of critics have commented on the name Hans Iver. The first was Hans Harbeck—"Hans Iver," *Der Freihafen, Blätter der Hamburger Kammerspiele*, I (1919), Heft 6, pp. 93–95. He notes, as do the others, that the name is almost identical with that of Hans Iwer, the werewolf in a poem by Klaus Groth which bears the name as its title—Klaus Groth, *Quickborn, Volksleben in plattdeutschen Gedich-*

ten ditmarscher Mundart, ed. K. Müllenhoff, 6th ed. (Hamburg, 1856), pp. 139–41. Klaus Groth was Barlach's favorite dialect poet, and there is little doubt that the poem is the source of the name. Harbeck explains the connection between the poem and the drama on the basis of a footnote (p. 139) by the editor Müllenhoff on local werewolf superstition. Müllenhoff writes: "According to popular belief, a werewolf, i.e., a person who goes around as a wolf at times—which is considered evil magic but also an incurable affliction—must assume his natural form again as soon as he is recognized and called by his right name, and is then doomed to die. . . ." Far easier than trying, as Harbeck does, to show that Fräulein Isenbarn calls Iver by his right name and releases him from his curse is to note that Iver, with his tendency to see himself reflected in others, accuses them of being wolves and of sucking his blood (*Dramen*, pp. 152–53).

21. *Ibid.*, p. 161.
22. *Ibid.*, p. 99.
23. *Ibid.*, p. 101.
24. *Ibid.*, p. 108.
25. *Ibid.*, pp. 149, 114, 112 f., 173.
26. *Ibid.*, p. 173.
27. *Ibid.*, p.177.
28. *Ibid.*, p. 182.
29. *Ibid.*, p. 105.
30. *Briefe*, I, 64.
31. Cf. *Briefe*, I, 47.
32. *Dramen*, p. 173.
33. *Ibid.*, p. 128.
34. *Ibid.*, pp. 132, 140, 144, 156, 172.
35. *Ibid.*, p. 172.
36. *Ibid.*, p. 182.
37. *Vierzig Fragen von der Seele* (1620), Frage 12.
38. *Dramen*, p. 128.
39. *Ibid.*, p. 100.
40. *Ibid.*, p. 183; *Briefe*, I, 59.
41. See above, p. 35.
42. *Briefe*, II, 156.
43. *Prosa*, II, 289.
44. *Prosa*, I, 327.
45. *Briefe*, II, 156.
46. *Prosa*, I, 334.
47. *Briefe*, II, 136.
48. "Dr. Eisenbart" (1899) in *Prosa*, I, 170–73.
49. *Ibid.*, p. 212.

50. *Ibid.*, p. 213.
51. *Ibid.*, p. 204 f., 210.
52. *Ibid.*, p. 103–4; cf. Goethe's *Faust,* lines 3845–46.
53. *Ibid.*, p. 242.
54. *Ibid.*, p. 241.
55. *Ibid.*, p. 242–43.
56. *Ibid.*, p. 241.
57. *Ibid.*, p. 268.
58. *Ibid.*, p. 271.
59. *Ibid.*, p. 273.
60. *Briefe*, II, 136.
61. *Prosa*, II, 380.
62. *Prosa*, I, 288.
63. *Theorie des modernen Dramas* (Frankfurt, 1959), p. 92.

Chapter Three

1. *Comedy,* Doubleday Anchor Books A 87 (Garden City, 1956), pp. 53–55. Parts of this chapter have appeared in *Modern Language Quarterly*, XX (1959), pp. 173–80 and are here reprinted by permission of the editors.
2. *Briefe*, I, 28.
3. *Briefe*, II, 122.
4. Alfred Kubin, *Die andere Seite,* 5th ed. (Munich/Berlin, n.d.), p. LXI.
5. *Ibid.*, p. 261.
6. *Ibid.*, p. 148.
7. *Briefe*, II, 121, 142.
8. *Ibid.*, p. 114.
9. *Ibid.*, p. 58–59.
10. *Ibid.*, p. 78.
11. Reproduced in Wolfgang Michel, *Das Teuflische und das Groteske in der Kunst* (Munich, 1919), p. 21.
12. Published in 1922 by Cassirer in Berlin.
13. *Vorschule der Aesthetik*, Erste Abteilung, §35.
14. *Origin of Attic Comedy* (London, 1914), pp. 81, 57, 84 ff.
15. *Dramen*, p. 201.
16. Henri Bergson, "Laughter," *Comedy*, Doubleday Anchor Books A 87 (Garden City, 1956), p. 93.
17. *Dramen*, p. 219.
18. *Ibid.*, p. 222.
19. *Ibid.*, p. 187.
20. The mother of the illegitimate child may be his daughter. The

driver has overheard Gierhahn making disrespectful comments about
her just before he leaves to do his bloody deed.

21. *Dramen*, p. 238.
22. *Ibid.*, p. 248.
23. *Ibid.*, p. 250.
24. *Ibid.*, p. 265.
25. *Ibid.*, p. 251.
26. *Ibid.*, p. 245.
27. *Ibid.*, p. 245.
28. *Ibid.*, p. 265.
29. *Briefe*, I, 77.
30. *Dramen*, p. 143.
31. *Ibid.*, p. 149.
32. *Ibid.*, pp. 219–20.
33. *Ibid.*, p. 147.
34. *Ibid.*, p. 152.
35. *Das Teuflische*, p. 67.
36. *Briefe*, II, 221.
37. *Briefe*, I, 55.
38. *Dramen*, p. 269.
39. *Ibid.*, p. 299.
40. *Ibid.*, pp. 314–15.
41. *Ibid.*, p. 312.
42. *Prosa*, I, 345.
43. *Ibid.*, p. 342.
44. Wolfgang Kayser in *Das Groteske: Seine Gestaltung in Malerei
und Dichtung* (Oldenburg/Hamburg, 1957), p. 189, asserts; "Es geht
beim Grotesken nicht um Todesfurcht, sondern um Lebensangst."
45. *Prosa*, I, 349.
46. *Ibid.*, p. 337.
47. *Ibid.*, p. 355.
48. *Comedy*, p. 107.
49. *Dramen*, p. 147.
50. *The Ludicrous Demon*, University of California Publications in
Modern Philology, No. 71 (Berkeley and Los Angeles, 1963).
51. Kenneth Burke, *Attitudes toward History*, I (New York, 1937),
p. 75.
52. *The Ludicrous Demon*, p. 22.
53. *Dramen*, pp. 190, 245.
54. *The Ludicrous Demon*, p. 18.
55. *Briefe*, II, 178.
56. *Ernst Barlach* (Gütersloh, 1957), pp. 50–51.

57. *Theaterprobleme* (Zürich, 1955), p. 48.

58. Charles Baudelaire, "On the Essence of Laughter," *Mirror of Art: Critical Studies,* tr. and ed. by Jonathan Mayne, Doubleday Anchor Books A 84 (Garden City, 1956), p. 143.

Chapter Four

1. See Helmut Krapp, "Der allegorische Dialog," *Akzente* (1954), pp. 210–19; and Horst Wagner, "Barlach: *Die Sündflut,*" in *Das deutsche Drama,* ed. Benno von Wiese, 2nd ed. (Düsseldorf, 1960), II, 338–56. Parts of this chapter have appeared in *The Germanic Review,* XXXIII (1958), pp. 243–50.

2. *Briefe,* II, 125.

3. *Barlach im Gespräch,* aufgezeichnet von Friedrich Shult (Wiesbaden; Insel-Verlag, 1948), p. 17.

4. *Briefe,* II, 157.

5. *Dramen,* p. 383.

6. *Briefe,* II, 142.

7. *Ibid.,* p. 104.

8. *Expressionismus,* eds. H. Friedmann and O. Mann (Heidelberg, 1956), p. 340.

9. Hans Schwerte, "Über Barlachs Sprache," *Akzente* (1954), pp. 219–25; Elisabeth Lichter, "Wort und Bild in den Dramen Ernst Barlachs," unpubl. diss. (Heidelberg, 1960).

10. *Dramen,* p. 583.

11. *Briefe,* I, 62.

12. *Ibid.,* p. 63.

13. *Expressionismus,* p. 308.

14. *Dramen,* p. 346.

15. *Ibid.,* p. 324.

16. *Ibid.,* p. 363.

17. *Dramen,* p. 340.

18. *Ibid.,* p. 380.

19. *Ibid.,* p. 325.

20. *Ibid.,* p. 348.

21. *Ibid.,* p. 340.

22. *Ibid.,* p. 324.

23. *Ibid.,* p. 344.

24. *Ibid.,* pp. 325, 340, 357.

25. *Ibid.,* p. 360.

26. *Ibid.,* p. 326.

27. *Ibid.,* p. 326.

28. *Ibid.,* p. 322.

29. *Ibid.*, p. 325.
30. *Ibid.*, p. 324.
31. *Ibid.*, p. 373.
32. *Ibid.*, p. 346.
33. *Ibid.*, pp. 349–51.
34. *Ibid.*, p. 344.
35. *Ibid.*, pp. 367, 368.
36. *Ibid.*, p. 372.
37. *Ibid.*, p. 377.
38. *Ibid.*, p. 370.
39. *Briefe*, I, 40.
40. *Briefe*, II, 121, 142.
41. *Prosa*, II, 552.
42. *Briefe*, II, 156–57, 178, 182.
43. *Briefe*, II, 178.
44. *Ibid.*, p. 136.
45. *Ibid.*, pp. 71, 178.
46. *Dramen*, p. 514.
47. *Ibid.*, p. 551.
48. *Ibid.*, p. 619.

Chapter Five

1. I. W. Lucas, " 'Der blaue Boll' and the New Man," *German Life and Letters*, XVI (1963), 238–47. Parts of this chapter have appeared in the *Germanic Review*, XL (1965), 31–40.
2. Nuremberg, 1963.
3. *Ibid.*, p. 120.
4. *Dramen*, p. 455.
5. *Briefe*, III, 99.
6. *The Unmediated Vision* (New Haven, 1954), pp. 128–29.
7. When the Herr repeats a phrase spoken by Mephistopheles in Goethe's *Faust*, Boll calls him "a practiced Satan" (*Dramen*, p. 454).
8. *Briefe*, II, 135.
9. *Dramen*, pp. 391–92.
10. *Ibid.*, p. 455.
11. *Ibid.*, p. 446.
12. *Ibid.*, p. 446.
13. *Ibid.*, pp. 447–48.
14. *Ibid.*, p. 448.
15. *Ibid.*, p. 452.
16. I. W. Lucas, p. 242.
17. *Briefe*, III, 82.

18. *Dramen*, p. 162.

19. Compare the passages on "augenscheinlich gemachte Weltseele" in *Prosa*, I, 334, 406.

20. *Dramen*, p. 387.

21. *Ibid.*, p. 388.

22. *Ibid.*, p. 395.

23. *Ibid.*, pp. 397–401.

24. *Ibid.*, p. 404.

25. *Ibid.*, p. 421

26. *Ibid.*, p. 444.

27. *Briefe*, II, 71.

28. *Dramen*, p. 433.

29. See Chapter Two; and *Prosa*, I, 334.

30. *Dramen*, pp. 24, 85.

31. *Ibid.*, p. 54.

32. *Ibid.*, p. 72.

33. *Ibid.*, p. 279.

34. *Prosa*, II, 483.

35. *Ibid.*, p. 504.

36. *Prosa*, I, 363.

37. *Ibid.*, p. 356.

38. *Ibid.*, p. 406.

39. *Ibid.*, p. 358.

40. *Ibid.*, p. 405.

41. *Ibid.*, p. 375.

42. *Ibid.*, pp. 387, 437.

43. *Ibid.*, p. 413.

44. *Ibid.*, p. 457.

45. *Ibid.*, p. 466.

46. This assumes that the six loose pages found in Book Two of the manuscript contain at least the essence of the Dialog. *Prosa*, I, 501–4.

47. *Ibid.*, pp. 466–67.

48. *Briefe*, II, 75.

49. *Prosa*, II, 367.

50. *Briefe*, II, 156. See also pp. 73, 78, 89; and *Briefe*, I, 59.

51. *Ibid.*, p. 78.

52. *Ibid.*, p. 177.

53. *Briefe*, III, 96.

54. *Prosa*, II, 453.

55. *Ibid.*, p. 462.

56. *Ibid.*, p. 553.

57. *Ibid.*, p. 503.

58. *Ibid.*, p. 462.

59. *Ibid.*, p. 463.

Chapter Six

1. *Briefe*, II, 75.

2. *Ibid.*, pp. 36–37.

3. *Ibid.*, p. 34.

4. *Ibid.*, p. 83.

5. *Briefe*, I, 50; *Gespräch*, p. 18.

6. *Gespräch*, p. 18.

7. *Briefe*, I, 62–63.

8. "Ich möchte, . . . Ihren Absichten förderlich und dienstlich sein" (*Dramen*, p. 454). Cf. *Faust*, I, l. 2664.

9. *Briefe*, I, 78, and Reinhard Piper, *Mein Leben als Verleger* (Munich, 1964), p. 436.

10. *Prosa*, II, 367–85.

11. *Ibid.*, p. 380.

12. "Konto Kollmann" and "Nachruf für Albert Kollmann" in *Prosa*, II, 385–92.

13. Piper, p. 423.

14. Piper, p. 430.

15. *Briefe*, II, 16.

16. *Ibid.*, pp. 83 ff. Erich Neumann, *Ursprungsgeschichte des Bewußtseins* (Zurich, 1949), pp. 183–87. The translation is taken from *The Origins and History of Consciousness*, I, tr. R. F. C. Hull, Harper Torchbooks TB 2007 (New York, 1962), p. 168.

17. *Briefe*, II, 86.

18. *Ibid.*, p. 142.

19. Paul Böckmann, *Formgeschichte der deutschen Dichtung*, I (Hamburg, 1949), 218.

20. *Dramen*, p. 415.

21. See Naomi Jackson, "Ernst Barlach. The Development of a Versatile Genius," unpubl. diss. (Radcliffe, 1950), pp. 434 ff. for a long treatment of the parallels between *Faust* and *Der blaue Boll*.

22. Goethe, *Die Leiden des jungen Werthers*, Book I, Letter of August 18th.

23. See Wolfgang Martens, *Bild und Motiv im Weltschmerz* (Cologne/Graz, 1957).

24. *Dramen*, pp. 135, 136, 150.

25. Richard Wagner, "Oper und Drama," in *Sämtliche Dichtungen und Schriften*, 5th ed. (Leipzig, n.d.), III. Teil, Band IV, 132.

26. *Geschlossene und offene Form in Drama* (Munich, 1960).

27. "Groteskformen des Theaters," *Akzente*, VII (1960), pp. 321–39.

28. See Eduard Berend, "Die Personen- und Ortsnamen in Jean Pauls Werken," *Hesperus*, XIV (October, 1957), pp. 21–31.

29. *Dramen*, p. 392.

30. Max Kommerell, *Jean Paul*, 3rd ed. (Frankfurt, 1957), pp. 354, 304.

31. Kommerell, p. 338.

32. See Hermann Villiger, "Jean Pauls humoristische Sprache," *Trivium*, III (1945), 81–98.

33. "Jugendstil in der Lyrik," *Akzente*, IV (1957), 28.

34. Elisabeth Klein (b. Kehrer), "Jugendstil in deutscher Lyrik," unpubl. diss. (Cologne, 1957).

35. *Über den Jugendstil und andere Essays* (Hamburg, 1956), pp. 19–20.

36. Elisabeth Klein, p. 74.

37. *Dramen*, p. 182.

38. *Ibid.*, p. 173.

39. See *Dramen*, p. 181.

40. *Prosa*, I, 328–30; *Prosa*, II, 351–52.

41. "Ernst Barlach und das Problem der Form," unpubl. diss. (Münster, 1955).

42. See Naomi Jackson's dissertation, pp. 385 ff.

43. *Prosa*, II, 701.

44. *Briefe*, II, 75; *Gespräch*, p. 19.

45. E.g., Barlach and Nietzsche, Barlach and Brecht, Barlach and "Plattdeutsch" Poetry.

46. *Briefe*, I, 50.

Chapter Seven

1. This chapter owes a large debt to the critical and collecting efforts of others, particularly to the Barlach-Archiv in Hamburg and to Dietrich Fleischauer, whose "Barlach auf der Bühne, eine Inszenierungsgeschichte" (Diss., Cologne, 1955) is full of valuable details and statistics. The greater part of this chapter appeared in *The German Quarterly*, XXXVI (1963), pp. 29–51, and is reprinted here with the permission of the editors.

2. Alfred Kerr, "Aussichten der Sprechbühne," *Neue Rundschau*, XXXVIII, Pt. 1 (1927), p. 68. Many years later, in 1934, Barlach looked back with some good humor on Kerr's unreasoned hostility and wrote: "Kerr, my bad friend, never did make this joke or malicious witticism, saying: Barlach is 'lachbar' (ludicrous), I have been watching for it for years" (*Briefe*, II, 204).

3. *Zehn unveröffentlichte Briefe Ernst Barlachs an Prof. Dr. Karl*

Notes and References

Weimann, ed. Anneliese and Hans Harmsen, Barlach-Gesellschaft, Gabe zum 2. Januar 1961.

4. *Briefe*, II, 95.

5. *Briefe*, I, 49.

6. Karl Barlach, *Mein Vetter Ernst Barlach* (Bremen, 1960), pp. 63–64.

7. *Briefe*, II, 142.

8. *Ibid.*, p. 102.

9. *Ibid.*, pp. 103–4. In the following vehement excerpt from an unpublished letter, quoted here from Flieschhauer's "Barlach auf der Bühne," p. 12, he repeats his reasons: "Himmel, ist das nicht wahr, daß vor einem schematisierten Bühnenbild der agierende, feuerspeiende, Schritte zu Boden stampfende Mensch ein Pfürzlein ist?"

10. *Gespräch*, p. 17.

11. *Briefe*, I, 53.

12. Alfred Kerr, "Rückschau, Vorschau," *Neue Rundschau*, XXXII (1921), Pt. 2, 960.

13. Julius Bab, *Das Theater der Gegenwart* (Leipzig, 1928), p. 184.

14. Reinhard Piper, *Mein Leben als Verleger* (Munich, 1964), p. 423.

15. Typescript dated Berlin-Grunewald, Oktober, 1954, and signed: Eggers-Kestner; in the files of the Barlach-Archiv, Hamburg.

16. *Berliner Börsen-Kurier*, May 20, 1935.

17. *Deutsche Allgemeine Zeitung*, May 20, 1935.

18. Photocopy of a newspaper review found in the Barlach Archiv. Probably *Berliner Tageblatt*, April 5 or 6, 1925.

19. Review signed "R. B." in the *Stuttgarter Zeitung*, March 15, 1954.

20. *Rheinischer Merkur*, March 19, 1954.

21. Review signed "g. g." in the *Hamburger Allgemeine*, October 8, 1946.

22. Herbert Ihering, *Von Reinhardt bis Brecht*, I (Berlin, 1958), p. 319.

23. *Die Weltbühne*. Der Schaubühne XIX. Jahr (1923), p. 642.

24. Willy Haas, *Die literarische Welt* (Munich, 1957), p. 147.

25. Photocopy of a review by Wilhelm Westecker dated December 8, 1930; in the Barlach-Archiv.

26. Friedrich-Karl Kobbe in the *Hamburger Nachrichten*, March 27, 1934.

27. These remarks do not apply to the very adequate performances in 1961 at the Berlin Schillertheater.

28. *Rheinischer Merkur*, December 12, 1953.

29. *Hamburger Anzeiger*, May 20, 1935.

30. *Berliner Börsen-Kurier,* May 20, 1935.

31. Review in *Die Kommenden,* Neue Folge, June 20, 1935.

32. Paul Fechter, *Das europäische Drama,* II (Mannheim, 1957), p. 539.

33. *Loc. cit.*

34. Bruno E. Werner in the *Deutsche Allgemeine Zeitung,* May 20, 1935.

Selected Bibliography

Primary Sources

The seven dramas and *A Self-Told Life* which appeared in print during Barlach's lifetime were published by Paul Cassirer, Berlin, between 1912 and 1929. The text of *Der Graf von Ratzeburg*, based on a preliminary draft dated 1927, was published posthumously in 1951 by the Grillen-Presse, Hamburg. The definitive manuscript version disappeared in 1945.

The Dead Day (*Der tote Tag*), 1912.
The Poor Relation (*Der arme Vetter*), 1918.
The Genuine Sedemunds (*Die echten Sedemunds*), 1920.
The Foundling (*Der Findling*), 1922.
The Flood (*Die Sündflut*), 1924.
The Blue Mr. Boll (*Der blaue Boll*), 1926.
A Self-Told Life (*Ein selbsterzähltes Leben*), 1928.
The Good Time (*Die gute Zeit*), 1929.

The three-volume Piper edition of the poetic work (Munich, 1956–59) contains not only everything Barlach published during his lifetime but also a generous selection from the literary remains: diaries, sketches, notebooks, uncompleted manuscripts.

BARLACH, ERNST. *Das dichterische Werk, Vol. I: Die Dramen*, ed. Klaus Lazarowicz and Friedrich Droß. Munich, 1956.

——. *Das dichterische Werk, Vol. II: Die Prosa I*, ed. Friedrich Dross. Munich, 1958.

——. *Das dichterische Werk, Vol. III: Die Prosa II*, ed. Friedrich Droß; "Nachwort" by Walter Muschg. Munich, 1959.

——. *Aus seinen Briefen*, ed. Friedrich Dross. Munich, 1947.

——. *Leben und Werk in seinen Briefen*, ed. Friedrich Droß. Munich, 1952.

——. *Frühe und späte Briefe*, eds. Paul Schurek and Hugo Sieker. Hamburg, 1962.

——. *Barlach im Gespräch*, aufgezeichnet von Friedrich Schult. Wiesbaden: Insel-Verlag, 1948.

————. *Three Plays by Ernst Barlach,* tr. Alex Page. Minneapolis, 1964.

STUDIES

1. *Mostly Biographical*

BARLACH, KARL. *Mein Vetter Ernst Barlach.* Bremen, 1960. Full of interesting details, the product of a lifelong, close friendship between cousins with common interests.

FRANCK, HANS. *Ernst Barlach: Leben und Werk.* Stuttgart, 1961. Admittedly preliminary to a definitive work. Journalistic in style. Subjective views. Yet very informative.

PIPER, REINHARD. *Mein Leben als Verleger.* Munich, 1964. Piper devotes rather long sections of his rambling autobiography to his friend Barlach.

SCHUREK, PAUL. *Begegnungen mit Barlach: Ein Erlebnisbericht.* Munich, 1959. A Güstrow friend records his and others' recollections. Particularly good on Barlach's last years.

2. *Mostly Critical*

FECHTER, PAUL. *Ernst Barlach.* Gütersloh, 1957. Devotes a long chapter to Barlach the writer. Suggestive but diffuse.

FLEISCHHAUER, DIETRICH. "Barlach auf der Bühne: Eine Inszenierungsgeschichte." Diss. Cologne, 1955. A thorough account of what happened to Barlach's plays on the stage and how the critics reviewed them.

FLEMMING, WILLI. *Ernst Barlach: Wesen und Werk.* Sammlung Dalp, No. 88. Berne, 1958. A comprehensive treatment of Barlach's graphic work, sculpture, writings, and thought. Sure in its critical judgments. Valuable summaries and paraphrases.

HOLLMANN, WERNER. "Das religiöse Erlebnis bei Ernst Barlach." *Monatshefte,* XLI (1950), 1–8. Describes the various kinds of religious experience in the dramas.

JACKSON, NAOMI. "Ernst Barlach: The Development of a Versatile Genius." Diss. Radcliffe, 1950. A full and enthusiastic discussion of all phases of his work. Points out many parallels and possible influences.

JUST, KLAUS GÜNTHER. "Ernst Barlach." *Deutsche Dichter der Moderne,* ed. Benno von Wiese (Berlin, 1965), pp. 400–419. An important and astonishingly full treatment of Barlach's life and three best plays within the allotted space. Good bibliography.

KEITH-SMITH, BRIAN. "Ernst Barlach," in *German Men of Letters,* ed. Alex Natan. London, 1964. III, 55–81. Contains a good biographical sketch. Otherwise uneven and occasionally inaccurate.

Selected Bibliography

LICHTER, ELISABETH. "Wort und Bild in den Dramen Ernst Barlachs." Diss. Heidelberg, 1960. Careful, systematic discussion, marred only by some abstruse terminology.

LUCAS, I. W. "Barlach's 'Der blaue Boll' and the New Man." *German Life and Letters,* XVI (1963), 238–47. Views Barlach in the context of late expressionism.

McFARLANE, J. W. "Plasticity in Language: Some Notes on the Prose Style of Ernst Barlach." *Modern Language Review,* XLIX (1954), 451–60. Good on *Seespeck* and spatial relationships.

MANN, OTTO. "Ernst Barlach." *Expressionismus: Gestalten einer literarischen Bewegung,* eds. Hermann Friedmann and Otto Mann (Heidelberg, 1956), pp. 296–313. An archconservative literary historian dwells somewhat disapprovingly on Barlach's religious ideas and dramatic form.

MEIER, HERBERT. *Der verborgene Gott: Studien zu den Dramen Ernst Barlachs.* Nuremberg, 1963. Philosophically oriented.

MUSCHG, WALTER. *Die Zerstörung der deutschen Literatur.* 3rd ed. Berne, 1958. Muschg (d. 1965) has given by far the best critical appreciations of Barlach. This volume contains two of these. The third is the "Nachwort" to Volume III of *Das dichterische Werk.*

SCHWEITZER, HEINZ. *Ernst Barlachs Roman "Der gestohlene Mond."* Baseler Studien zur deutschen Sprache und Literatur, No. 22. Berne, 1959. Contains a good section on the language.

SCHWERTE, HANS. "Über Barlachs Sprache." *Akzente* (1954), p. 219–25. Short but full of significant insights.

WAGNER, HORST. "Barlach: *Die Sündflut.*" *Das deutsche Drama,* ed. Benno von Wiese. 2nd ed. Düsseldorf, 1960. II, 338–56. A close study of a single play.

WELLIVER, GLENN E. "Internal Evidence of the Interrelation of Ernst Barlach's Dramas." Diss. Northwestern, 1964.

Index

Index